The Process: Living the singles journey as it happens

The Process: Living the singles journey as it happens

THE PROCESS

Living the Singles Journey as it Happens

By Faith S Dore

The Process: Living the singles journey as it happens

DEDICATION

This book is dedicated to all the single individuals across the world, young and old, male and female.

To those who have embraced their single journey and to those who have not quite been able to do so.

To those who feel their hearts cannot love again, to those who long to be loved.

There is a quote I love to hear, which is this: "Love requires a leap of faith". [1]

I know this journey for some of you may not be as easy as it may seem for others that you may know. It can also be really hard and testing I must say, but I can only hope that if you are willing to learn and grow with me in this season, you will be waiting with great expectation, patiently with hope for your spouse to come.

So get your suitcase or backpacks ready, your passports/ID in check and let's set off on this single journey together.

---

1. Quote: From A December Bride – Film: Director – David Winning, Writers – Denise Hunter and Karen Berger (2016)

The Process: Living the singles journey as it happens

CONTENTS

Faith S Dore

ACKNOWLEDGEMENTS

Firstly, I would like to thank God for his faithfulness, peace, unconditional love and acceptance he has towards me, sustaining and enabling me to have this vision and dream to write such a book as this, in such a testing season of my life.

To my dearest mum; relationships were never really something I could easily talk to you about, but as we went through drastic seasons of change, you helped me with the boldness installed through Christ Jesus to open up to you and be as honest as I can be. Thank you for opening the door and providing your listening ears, fervent prayers, caring advice and warm love.

To my family and dear friends who have endured my complaints, watched my tears, and stood back when I needed to be taught a lesson, comforted me when I needed it and most of all always had my back in prayers and many more ways, THANK YOU.

To my dad who didn't get to see me write nor complete my book, I miss you and hope I have made you proud.

And finally to the one I call my husband-to-be whom I may or may not have met yet, thanks for being a hope, a dream, a heartfelt desire, a glimpse of reality that I know one day I will see face to face, I am looking forward to knowing you and to experiencing all the great adventures to come together. PS: I like you.

The Process: Living the singles journey as it happens

INTRODUCTION

Singleness, where does anyone really begin with such a topic as this? It's almost like opening Pandora's Box and finding things that revolve around one word: Single. There are so many thoughts, funny stories, memories good and not so good ones that come to mind. But, who really has a choice but to meddle deeper or run away into finding ourselves in our singleness?

I think it's fair to say that we can all tell a few stories from our 'single' experience, not forgetting the stories from our friends and family lives too. Why? Because at some point in each of our lives we have been on or still are on this journey.

Come on, who doesn't like a love story, even if it's not your own, I know I loved watching the Royal Wedding of Prince Harry and Meghan. What a beautiful ceremony, they are so cute together, (in my view), however, I still asked the small question, when is it going to be my turn?

This book isn't a vent book, but rather I hope it's a book you can highly relate too. I hope we can be real with each other, and just maybe shed a bit of light, clarity, point out things you may not have understood or even given a thought to. So who knows, you may just get an 'Aha' moment.

The Process: Living the singles journey as it happens

Life has a funny way of teaching each one of us lessons and giving insight. It can, at times feel dramatic, or even uncomfortable. But I guess the question is, are we willing to learn the lessons thrown at us either through our own experiences or that of others?

I may not know everything, let alone 100% as to what you are going through or have been through in your single journey, so I truly do not consider myself a 'single guru', - ha, if such a thing even exists. But what I do know is that there is going to be something within these chapters that will make you say 'oh my gosh, that's so true or no wayyy!'

You may cry, you may laugh, or you may just heal.

Whatever your reaction, I pray it's a blessing and a joy to go through these pages and if you picked up this book, then I believe there is something about your single journey that you can reflect on or relate to.

Please remember singleness is not a curse, neither are you to be seen as an outcast just because you are single. Singleness to me as I will explain in this book is an open opportunity to grow and find who you really are, discovering your purpose and also what you are able to bring positively into a healthy relationship, and ultimately to marriage.

With that being said, let's continue this journey together and let's see what we can discover along the way.

Ready?

Let's go.

Happy Reading.

CHAPTER 1

HELLO SINGLE WORLD

1. Here we go

I t's almost like I was given an invitation that said: *"Welcome to the world of singleness, where the next date is not promised, but a hope, a dream or sometimes fear of being unaccepted may show its face or be birthed…"* My response…Blah.

This invitation I started to realise was one that I could not say no to, I felt the other alternative was to settle and be in any relationship for the sake of it, or just so I could update my 'status' to be 'in a relationship' because everyone else around me seemed to be in a relationship.

Since I broke up with my ex 11 years ago, I guess no one had really, truly seen me yet. So then singleness for me became my home…Yipiiiiie, not (yep, that's me being sarcastic).

I've been asked numerous times about my dating life or 'anyone you interested in?' type of questions by prying friends and family, which my answer then becomes…Nope, which is then followed by them having this reaction, especially when they know how long you have been single for: 'Ohhhh'(Big eye opened moment) or with that slight look of concern. Tell me why?

But then I also hear the other response of those that are in similar journeys or even longer as myself, they say it can even get to a point where a big conversation and further questioning comes out as to why we are still single. Which, of course, if we knew, we would have been able to give a more straightforward answer as they hoped. Ha, Story.

So tell me, what is the true solution to this journey of LOVE especially from a singles perspective, what does true love really look like and how is it found?

You see my single's journey has not been a great experience, to be honest with you, it's been a battle with both the triumph rounds in the ring, as well as some knocked out rounds...Yi, Yi, Yi.
I have been very emotional at times, I have learned a little here and there, written in my journal my thoughts from time to time, (I have always heard that it's good to write your feelings down to express yourself). I have also complained or to be frank, moaned a lot to my dear cousins and friends, whom most of the times have been humble, understanding and willing to listen.

But then my spiritual side of things, I pray a lot to God. You know those prayers: *"Why am I still single?"* *"Where is he, wake him up, let me see him and let him see me"* kind of prayers, and as much as I do believe that God has been hearing me and still hears me, I tend to also pray as the man in the Bible did (Mark 9:24) *"Lord I believe, But reality is telling me otherwise, so help me with my unbelief"* (Paraphrased).

I realised, as time went by that things started to change from 2008/9 – 2015/6. I was kind of in the same mindset, feeling sorry for myself, attending weddings, parties etc. Hoping to 'find my man there'.....nope, trying to settle for the sake of being liked, whilst losing my own sense of worth and even thinking that God doesn't care about me or does, but only to a certain extent, it almost felt like I was forgotten. Huh, go figure.

But surely LOVE should not be this much of a struggle right?

Okay, please tell me you can relate because I don't want you to feel left out at this early stage. You know those moments when all your male friends seem to be finding their ladies, but you wonder deep down if you are going to be good enough or even find that 'down for you' type of lady. Yep, that right there is what I am talking about.

There were songs that were on constant repeat on my playlist like, 'You are not forgotten' by Israel Houghton, 'Every prayer' by Israel Houghton feat Mary Mary or 'Fragile Heart' and 'Only if God says yes' by Yolanda Adams, plus one of my ultimate favourites 'Alabaster box' by CeCe Winans. I mentioned this to say that I felt that I needed these songs to at least try to pick me up from the 'single down out pit' I dragged myself into, but to be honest, there were times when it did the opposite, it just made me at times feel worst, but why?

Why did singleness start to feel like a curse rather than a season of growth or blessings?
I truly think when you are led by your emotions, what others say, especially on social media, and what you see around you combined with the unshakeable feeling deep down that you want to be loved, it can be so easy to start overthinking things and behaving in ways completely out of your character. Singleness becomes no longer a growing season, as I now understand it to be, but a 'down depressive' season.

Has your journey been any different? I'm sure it possibly has been, if not slightly the same.

Now don't get me wrong, I tried nearly everything to reject this single invitation. I knew I wanted to be loved and in a great relationship because I never really felt the love from a younger age. I guess you can say love was there but the love my parents and siblings gave was the 'tough type of love'. So I searched high and low, elsewhere for the 'soft/gentle' kind of love.

I even tried speed dating: BTW[2]: Not again! Just a quick insight into this....ha....Think about this, 20 women to about 9 guys....How? Some who didn't even want to be there, I mean as I talked to them, they started confessing that they were only there to support the organizer because apparently most of the guys 'dropped out' really? Come onnn I am trying to find a husband, not some type of 'cover-up' here!
There even came a point where I felt sorry for my friend who I went with, as she was sat on the last chair (how the numbers worked) so I had to waaaait a very long time for the final guy to reach her. By this time it was getting so late into the night and others started to go home....ha ha ha...so much for connecting.

We both left with no interest or dates, but reflection and laughter, and for that I am grateful. I guess something good can always come out of any situation you face especially if you dare yourself, step outside of your comfort zone, and feel uncomfortable or embarrassed. Take for instance

---

2. BTW: By the way

if we never went, we wouldn't know what the whole 'speed dating' experience was all about.

Getting back to what I was saying before, so despite speed dating, even online dating and all my other efforts, my mood seemed to be okay for a bit and then my mood went straight back to feeling down. I guess I just found it so hard to move on after my previous long relationship that I had invested in every way, which at the time lead to an engagement, then a breakup and no happy ending. I must admit it was not a great place to be in my life at the time.

LESSON

In this journey, I have learnt and I am still learning about myself, my likes, dislikes, values, worth, my type (of man/spouse?) and also what God is saying in this season of my life.
I believe life will always throw challenges our way, especially regarding relationships both intimate and non-intimate, but it's how we approach or deal with these challenges that really matter.

There was one day after work, where I sat and watched a beautiful love movie, I know, I know, yes I love them, guys some of you know you love these types of movies too, go on admit it, there is totally nothing to be ashamed about, (wink). This was called, **Love at first glance**. I was taught a lovely message and this is what was said: *Love is unexpected.*[3]

---

[3] Love at first glance: Director – Kevin Connor, Writers and Producer – Kathy Kloves (2017)

The Process: Living the singles journey as it happens

How many times have you heard the famous saying *"It's when you are not looking that's when love actually finds you?"* hmmm, interesting right? We'll definitely get a chance to go a little deeper into this, in Chapter 11.

PS: Have you ever heard of this other saying "you never really come out of the single world until you are officially married?" Mind blowing right?

I was shown this when I was doing my research on singleness over the years, I had joined a dating course at my church at the time to learn more about Christian dating/relationships and came to understand that in the Biblical times, the term 'dating' didn't actually exist, back then you just either 'courted' if you already knew a lady was the one for you, or one of the other common ways of old and present in different cultures is also known as arranged marriage.

Some today, through discussing this with friends have said that this possibly was a better way of finding love due to how difficult it is now, but as we know that may not be 100% true for all.

So tell me where does that leave us then today?

-Passing through <u>Journal</u> City -

CHAPTER 2

THE NOTES

2. Take time to write

Have you ever written letters to God or your 'spouse' in your diary, journal, or since technology has kicked in, on your phone or other electronic devices like notepad? If so, have you thought that just one day you will be able to look back at them and see how you have grown, or what strides you have taken since the point of writing?

Well, I have and can confirm I have taken notes as far back as 23.01.2011 to be precise.

Here you will see a few things that were running through my single mind, can you possibly relate?

(WARNING! There are many spelling mistakes ahead – read on to see why they were not corrected)

23 January 2011 16:06

"Life is always an up and down flow. But the truth and best advice is to keep ontop and never let situations bring you down. Things happene abs most of the time it's what we can't control. God is so patient with us but at times we take our own roads and then end up with the worst result. I can be a witness to that as right now I really feel like crap. I mean can I really be honest. I feel like I have nothing but knowing God brings so much joy and recolation to know and have a relationship with Him to the point of having everything.

Things we see, experience and maybe even participate in can make us feel thatbour self worth is nothing, but Go has created us all unqically. If we was the same as others then what difference would we need to make in this world and what would this world really be like?

God knew what he was doing when He created me and each and everyone if us in this world. The question is, are we going to aim and strive to move in the way God has called us and if so what are we doing about it now. Or are we going to make our own paths?

I know for me, alot of things need to change. But most important I know that I cannot do it alone. And I dontnknow where to start. I feel like a mess, through the pain of my ex, through the discommunications I have with my family especially my parents. My attitude has to change to be more postive and most of all humble. There are things that make me snap so easily and it's just nit right. Lord it's only you I can talk to. Who can I really trust in this world?

I pray my scares will heal and that somehow I will be completely healed as be able to love again, because right now I deep justice needs to made, but at the end of the day, who I'm I to judge?

I tried of judgeing and critizing others. I'm tried of being hurt and hurting others. I just want to follow peace with all men, just has my heavenly father has told me.

Lord, let me not just proclaim Christinanty, but to show the love & hope but most of all forgiviness to others as ou have showed me. Lord teach me have to REALLY FORGIVE and FORGET. I really don't want to hold any grudge towards others. I want to be able tk let go of the hurt ppl cause me and forgive just as You forgive me.

I don't want what others have. I want whatever you have for me. Nothing is real in this world without you. Lift you head up women, lift up tour head young man & know that God I here for you. We are not alone.

Feedom, love, care, forgive and hope is all in the arms of Jesus.

Stop chasing after everything you see. You might not have everything you want. But you have everything you need <Kirk

Franklin>"

To be honest, when I had to read over that to add it into here, it gave me an overwhelming feeling. Sometimes you just don't know where you were or how down or low you could have been if you didn't note it down, spelling mistakes and all. *(Notes without spelling errors, please refer to the back of the book)*

I'm sure through reading this over that I was in a low place of singleness, still trying to get over the hurt that my ex-boyfriend caused me, issues with seeing my self-worth and more. But I guess yet still I had a light of hope in which I am so grateful for my faith, knowing I am accepted and truly loved by God in the midst of rejection was my saving grace.

PS: As briefly mentioned above, I left all my spelling mistakes and errors to say, in me being real with you, nothing has ever been super perfect with neither me nor my single journey. At times when we are in the lowest state of our 'single' mindset, where we are not dating anyone or no one has showed us any interest, if not careful we tend not to focus on what we should be focusing on that is 'correct and true' instead we tend to focus on what is 'negative, incorrect and even may place ourselves in situation we wouldn't even think of being in, especially if our minds were in check. Therefore, as a result of this, we face the consequences of our somewhat self-pity actions.

So, at some points in our lives, we do need to get ourselves together, to reflect and to heal rather than become hurt further.

Moving on from this place, I ended up here, the following year, and check out what I wrote:

28 August 2012 16:06

"Sometimes I feel like God is trying to say to us: Stop looking at

I noticed if we are not cautious, our single walk can lead us to feel left out, jealous or fixated on the relationships of others; and yes, that exactly happened a few times to me hence the reason I believe for the note. I guess I got to a point where I wanted to be in a relationship so badly because my friends and family were in 'one' were and it hurt me to be the outsider or the 'loner'.
This single journey can really feel like you're constantly looking around for what others are up to and at times could result in you feeling like a loner, we will touch on this subject further in chapter 5.

But I also think that's why it's so important not to settle or constantly focus on what others have. BTW: There is nothing wrong with admiring others relationships, but at the same time, if you admire too much it can turn into being a dangerous thing when your site becomes more envious and jealous than being inspired.

In writing my next notes, this is where I got to, did I grow from the above note, or did I remain where I was? Take a look:

19th December 2012 22:56

"I wonder
It's funny Lord,
I ask you for a husband, I seek your ways and your face. I ask you to draw me deeper into love with you & I am happy to say, I finally feel your love & your care.

But Father I come back to what I said in the beginning, please tell me where my husband is?

I look at Joshua and think he seems like such an amazing person, got the looks, the eyes, height, the voice, from what I can see, the heart for you, sense of humor, a passion to serve and develop and also a family who loves you too.

To me he seems like the on point husband.

And I KNOW you have other 'Joshua's' out there but I don't understand how come you are not hooking me up?

If you could look at Adam and know he needed a help mate & then sent him Eve, how come it feels like you are not looking at me in that way.

Father, as you know, I've had my share of crazy, unfaithful, ungodly relationships and I don't want those no more. I want you so centred in every relationship I have especially when it comes to be and my husband.

For this reason that's why I look at Joshua sometimes and feel sad, cause I just long to be loved by the right person, your son, your child, your man that you have so moulded for me.

I know his out there and he might not be Joshua, but it's still a nice thought to think it could be. From what I see you haven't given me any signs, or confirmation regarding my husband so how do you expect me to feel Lord?

I'm your daughter looking for answers will you not speak to me.

It fears me to think that someone who is not what I like look wise will say God said your my wife, when deep down in my heart I know that you know me very well and have created me in such a unique way.

Father, if you said to Rachel that my husband will be a fine man, then I believe it and receive it.

Father, many thoughts come to mind, and as much as I trust that you will work everything out for my good and especially try to keep serving whilst taking my thoughts off this topic, it seems to gradually creep back into mind... Why is that Father?

Your Word says that you will give me the desires of my heart, but Father it seems like that particular one you have become silent. Will you not speak Lord, will you not come to my aid & rescue me from this thought of sadness which is meant to be of joy?

I know you can hear me & I know you can see me around this. The thought of that alone, alongside thinking that you don't want to move on my behalf regarding this is pretty upsetting to me.

I look up to you Lord and noone else, I truly love you with my whole heart and do not ever want to put anyone before you. You are my number 1 and I really mean it.
Father, will you not help me. I speak from my heart"

The year was coming towards an end and my emotions, thoughts; life was on a full high-speed roller-coaster, turbo mode. What in the world was happening to me and why?
I think at this point in my life, all sort of challenges started to surface, one after the other, for example, the one I mentioned earlier, well; here's some content to it. A man by the name of Bob decided to contact my brother and ask if I was dating anyone, why? Yes, of course, he was interested, but that's beside the point. He didn't even really know my brother to ask him such a question.

Bob used to visit my parents from time to time, my parents let's say were 'fond' of him, because he was from the same place as we were from, in Nigeria and had a steady job, etc. But from day one, I was sceptical, so I would normally stay upstairs in my room, no eye contact, no need for hellos, after all, he was my parents 'friend' not mines, and in all honesty, I wasn't interested to know him, as harsh as that may sound.

The crazy thing is that I knew I wasn't interested in him, from all I could hear about him. Yes, I know you have to know folks first for yourself before you should make those kinds of judgements, but in all fairness, I could say I was a pretty good judge of character.

Fast forward, we did actually meet in person, and what did I tell you. I was right. It was just not happening for me, I looked at him, he smiled and I don't know what it was, I just became annoyed, maybe because at the time I assumed his tactic with an addition to his somewhat off-putting behaviour, I just cannot explain it, you just had to be there. At one point when I was talking to mum about him, I was telling her that I was getting annoyed with his behaviour…Mum gave me a funny look and I said, *"don't even think about it"*. She smirked, you know the look those who care for you give you when they think they have found you your potential spouse….'Nah, sorry mum, not for me'.

Moving on, Bob decides to take the next step and speak to my parents in which he says, he believed that **God** said I was to be his wife….ha, sorry what? Wrong! Nope not me, and I think in all that conversation he was having with 'God' I was clearly left out because God didn't say anything to me along the same lines of what he was saying.

Let me pause here one minute.

Watch this: Just because someone may use the words 'God said', doesn't mean that God really said so. You need to do your own individual prayer, asks God to speak to you too, because if he can speak to others about something that involves you then surely he can speak to you about the same matter.

The funny thing in all of this is this; before Bob even spoke those above words to my parents, I remember feeling within me God saying to me these distinctive words: "Just because someone is going to come in my name and say you are for them, doesn't mean I have sent them". There you go, now that was my own confirmation. So I had the confidence to say 'No' to him, no matter how many scriptures he quoted, no matter how my parents even challenged me as to whether I really heard from God or not. I knew what I knew even until today that what God said to me was real, because even when I had my self-doubt, I asked God to show me further signs, confirmation etc., and yet still he did, with the same response, "I told you already, He is not for you". Boom settled.

Peace of mind started to flow, taking over any type of confusion, strife, and arguments with parents. Geeze.

Tell me something; if your companion is meant to, draw you closer to Christ then why on earth would that person try to bring confusion? Bob's tactics and way of doing things, caused arguments between my parents and I, to the point where I was questioning God and my trust in Him. And for me, that was a RED flag, a cautionary sign, a flashing light. Your spouse should not make you feel negative or distance you from your faith, family and friends; rather they should be encouraging you to pursue those very things. In my opinion, little did Bob know that at this point I was not in a healthy position to be ready for marriage, especially not after breaking up with my ex of whom I was previously engaged too.

This I know is where my faith and self-confidence had to come in and loneliness and settlement could not answer the door to such proposal as I would never have known what kind of crazy marriage that would have been. Phew, Good save God!

I mentioned this story to say this, in the reflection of my notes, it reminded me that God had me all this time and protected me from what could have been utter shambles or a disaster be it with my ex, Bob or even others. It gave me a clear perspective and urged me to want to seek God more so that I could continue to make the right choices in life and especially within this single journey.

So then I wrote this:

24th May 2013 19:04

"As I sit
Dear Father,
As I sit on this bus heading home. I think of all the possible blessings you can provide/shower unto me. Then I smile again because I know you can do even more than I can imagine.

I thank you that through all the challenges in my life you stood by me and gave me with will power to carry on, because as you know, it's been really hard at times.

I am not quite sure how and when you will bless me with all my heart desires but I am willing to wait, even though I don't really know how to hold on much longer. Please would you help me?

Father it gets a bit tiring seeing others blessed around whilst it seems like I am struggling or lacking big time. But as I realised & said yesterday, I say it again today, for you are NOT a God to lie & I know you are faithful to your word, especially knowing the fact that your time is perfect.

Please may I obey your voice when you tell me to keep waiting.

Father, please, no more tears of sorrow, no more crazy disappointments, Father I really need the joy that you gave promised me, the peace & also the favour, but most of all your GRACE.

Father please hear your daughter, please hear my hearts cry unto

My relationship with God develops and still develops today. Even though I had these internal battles from time to time, I started to learn that I needed to be more specific about what I would like to see in my husband, after all, it was God that birthed this desire in my heart to be married, and I had his words to back me: *"....let your request be made known unto God"* (Philippians 4:6 KJV).

To conclude this chapter I wrote this:

14th October 2013 02:18

"Father,
Is it not you that paves the way for me?
You open your arms for me to run to & feel your warm embrace, but yet still I know you love me but yet fill unloved. What is this feeling, does it make sense to you?
Should I not be satisfied with your love, but yet still I reach out for the love of another, your child, your son of whom you created just. For. Me?

I gaze & think, surely this is what you want for me? You looked upon Adam & thought it was only right for him to have a campion, & then came Eve!
Is this not your wish for me?
Oh to be really/truly loved is one of my greatest dreams. To be held, to be appreciated, to help & be helped. To share life with your son, that is truly after you heart.
But then it's never been about my will but yours. Have you called me to singleness, then why this feeling, why this bitter sweet pain?
Yet still if this is what you desire of me, then let it be. Give me the

strength to endure, take these feelings away.
But yet still my Lord, why do I feel this way?

Oh to be loved, to txt to chat to share to step into another world than mine & to reach out & help.
To be welcomed, appreciated, honoured, cherished & to show/share it back, to laugh, to pray, to support. Settling is NOT & will not ever be an option.

To be truly loved Lord. When is it my time/turn for my life to change & stop struggling for everything or in anything & claim these promises & blessings you have for me?

Surely I will wait for you Lord. Come to my rescue, see, hear my outcry of my heart, aid me where I hurt, heal where there are still wounds. Shape & mould me to be the best lady I can be.

To my love, I am yet still to see you. I still await my Lord to confirm in many ways whom you are, where you are. But until my Lord says yes, & nods His head in approval. I Can't Go nowhere with you.

So I sit here & wait!"

Ummm, reading this over, seems like I really bug out God with my singleness, in particular, wanting to be loved and truly accepted in a relationship, right?

I can 100% admit that for sure, He is the main one I talk to in all my notes as I didn't want to keep burdening my cousin or friends with the same stories, complaints or moans.

As I said in the beginning, it's been a struggle from time to time, I felt so taken over by my emotions and what was going on around me, it felt like I was being sucked up into a tunnel and all you can do is hope that there is a light to show you the way out. And believe you me, there is always a way out, you just got to hang in there and see it through.

LESSON

Writing things down allows you to express your feelings, reflect and to either identify your strengths and weaknesses which may need a little working on.

Upon reflection, you may find that you challenge yourself not to remain in certain ruts or negative mindset, even to a point of writing mistakes and declaration that you know you shouldn't be writing, but to continue to work on your self-worth, confidence, and values to become the best version of you for you and also for your spouse to come.

So if you haven't done so already, I dare you to get a journal and if you have one already, great, start to write a few things down now and see how it goes and then reflect on what you have written after a couple of months or a year to see what has improved, what has changed, may need to change or stay as it is, after all, you have a choice, choose to do right by yourself, rather than wrong.

PS: No-one has to know, nor read it unless you decide to share it with the world as I've done. (wink).

1st Stop: Honest Lane

CHAPTER 3

IT'S A STRUGGLE

See that's just it, its life, we are all human, and have individuals needs that need to be met, but **at the appointed time**. This doesn't take away also from the insights of LUST too. We need to be careful that our desires do not get so caught up with the appearance of lust when we are single that we tend to not even see ourselves slipping and falling into bed, or the arms that we know we are not meant to be in at all.

So I have chosen the life of abstinence. Where I reserved myself from indulging in sex and any temptation towards sex. Which also includes, if kissing can lead there, then bye, no thank you, I like you, but I pass (everyone's boundaries/weakness will be different of course). Then I saw myself having these three choices at this point of singleness:

1) Allow my imagination to run wild and develop in areas that it should not – *Wasn't to be an option.*
2) Shut it down (the thoughts) ASAP, like those moments when you shake your head like your shaking the thought out your mind. *Ha, like that even really works. Geeze.*
3) Pray (bring the struggle to God and ask him to help you, especially in controlling your desires, whilst turning that desire into a longing for God) – *Correct!*

Deep down, I truly believe that sex is solely intended for marriage and marriage alone as it not only brings the husband and wife intimately together but it also celebrates the fact that one has the ability to passionately love and be loved. Why would you want it any other way?

Sex for some may fill a hole or a void for the moment, but tell me, once that moment has passed, and the so-called 'fun' is over, what happens then? Will you be lost or found?

In the words of Jermain Stewart's song: *'we don't have to take our clothes off to have a good time oh no...'*[5]

Ladies and Gents, your worth is so much more than a condom, pill or a one night stand. Your worth is so much more than what people say. Your worth is **priceless**. So why not find ways to stimulate your brain and take your mind off sex, foreplay and whatever other sexual title you want to give it for now because there is so much I realised you can do out there in this big place we call world and it doesn't have to involve, sleeping around, possibly catching a sexually transmitted disease and more.

One of the hardest thing for me was knowing that after taking my Love Language test in October 2018 (which I highly recommend you all to do) I noticed that **Physical touch** was one of my top 5 results, but with that result also came **Quality of time**, **Acts of service** and others, which is just to show that sex and more (The Physical side of things) was not always everything, neither should it be especially in or outside of marriage, as I believe a marriage also needs to run on great communication, friendship, companionship, support, love, grace, trust, respect, forgiveness and much, much more.

Maybe a task for you can be to find what your sexual triggers are, that may easily set you off and begin to put things in place to avoid or disconnect from it, until the time of marriage.

For example, if you start dating someone after being single for a while and have such urges when you start dating you need to try and avoid always being alone with each other because of your attraction to each other's, create healthy agreed boundaries and stay true to them all, go on group dates etc. After all, if that person is really into you they will completely

---

5. Jermaine Stewart song from "Frantic Romantic: We don't have to take out clothes off - Songwriters: Narada Michael Walden / Preston W. Glass (1986)

understand and share in your views. But most of all don't have a fickle mind, keep at it, there is no point in deceiving yourself, as you know you better and can tell your weak points.

Our sexual desires will always be there because we were created to love and be loved. But that feeling and expression should not be misused or taken advantage off, especially in the wrong content of not being married. I do get that this may not have been an option for some individuals through no fault of their own and believe me I completely understand, but as I can heal, so can you and I can only pray that God will help you move past those bad and unkind experiences as he has helped me to do so too.

LESSON

Remember; respect yourself, your body; 1 Corinthians 6:19-20 *"Do you not know that your bodies are temples of the Holy Spirit, who is in you, whom you have received from God? You are not your own; you were bought at a price. Therefore honor God with your bodies."* , and your worth and if the person you're into cannot respect you in those ways and more, then maybe it's best you don't drop your single card for them just yet.

Moving forward in this area of singleness and more, how about we look forward to enjoying and sharing these special intimate moments with our spouses to be and keep it as a beautiful and authentic connection.

3.2 Microwave vs Oven baked

Have you ever heard of the term: Microwave and oven baked relationships? Or maybe you have heard it this way: Microwavable women/man vs oven baked women/man?

Either way, It goes like this; As we know in cooking or baking when hungry and want something fast or done quickly in a short amount of time, you tend to go to the easily cooked food (ready-made) option and throw it into the microwave and then Voila, its cooked, done. It may not be the best quality of food but it's edible.

However, on the other hand, if you're a bit like me, who prefers things to taste authentically real, you will try your best to make time and realise you may have previously marinated some chicken or peeled some potatoes and vegetables. You then place them into the oven, set the timer and then in about 30mins to 1hr or more your food is cooked, done, smelling really good.

By taking this food out of the oven vs the microwave, you notice that it is too hot, so you have to wait a bit before it cools down, but once cooled you tuck right into your lovely baked chicken, potatoes and vegetables...hmmmm...hungry yet? Lol *(Laugh Out Loud)*.

I know this is possibly whetting your appetite a little, especially if you're hungry reading this, but this is far from being a cookbook as you know. By now with the two above examples, you would have realised that I was not relating to food, rather relationships that we tend to choose to dip in or out of when single and yet still we should 'hunger' for that delicious well-cooked oven baked relationships.

Let's go a bit deeper. The microwaveable relationships can come across as the 'not too serious' relationships where individuals for the sake of timing and life, just jump into it to feel a void or a want, aka 'settle'.

The oven baked relationship has been something you may have been waiting for a while in your single walk but now becomes time to invest in.

The point I am trying to get at is this: Our choices matter, whether you have been single for 1 week or 1 year, your choice of who you pick should always matter.

Your single status could easily tell you to get with someone the microwavable way (ASAP) for the sake of doing so to fulfil the gap of loneliness that you may have been feeling for a while or a moment.

But I feel the consequence is that you may end up forcing yourself to be with someone you know you have no business getting involved with and instead of taking the time to 'bake' = 'heal' yourself from possible pass breakups or others reasons you find yourself stuck to the point that you could hold onto a relationship which is unhealthy for you and may most likely affect you even more long term.

Take for example this, I dated a guy in college; let's call him Tony. He was cool and sweet, bless him, and was very much interested in me. But I wasn't into him nor was I 100% attracted to him, but don't get me wrong he was alright.

We didn't really have much in common and to be honest I had not too long ago came out of another relationship.

I had explained this to Tony, but I guess he had his own reasons of wanting to be in a relationship and persisted, which I slightly, yes slightly admired. So I just gave in and started dating him, the wrong choice.

I do not even think this relationship lasted up to 2 months, let alone a month, before I started seeing certain characteristics I did not like such as paranoia, over questionings of where I was going and who I was going with to places…talk about 'dad' part two, no thanks.

I suddenly realised, this was not a relationship I needed to be in nor was it healthy to stay within, so yes, the relationship ended.

At this point, no longer being in a relationship again, 'singleness' waved its invitation card at me and for the first time in a long time, I gladly accepted it, again.

I did leave that relationship feeling bad, because truly he liked me, but mentally and emotionally I was not in the right state of mind to receive it, despite trying. Call this a rebound relationship, I don't know, but it wasn't right at all to be in.

Years down the line I had to call him, not to ask for him to come back, but to apologise as I did feel I needed to and I knew that this was not guilt speaking, but correction and humility. I knew I shouldn't have gone into a relationship with Tony, knowing I just came out of a previous relationship. He wanted to give 100% and I couldn't, I felt like I settled as harsh as that sounded and because he seemed so invested (what every lady at some point will realise they want without the 'overbearing' attitude) things were just not right. It is only until you mature and reflect on such things you come to realise you may have mistreated others. The Bible puts it this way: *"Do to others as you would have them do to you."* (Luke 6:31 KJV)

You see, you must have also heard the famous saying, 'hurt people, hurt people'. So I knew I had to put it right.

Sometimes it may feel so easy to jump into another relationship straight after the others and live the microwavable 'free' life, but as you can see from the relationship with Tony, a friendship was not really built, everything seemed rushed and characteristics were seen that I should not have entertained at all. But how was I meant to really know all this in the space of 1-2months? Especially with someone I barely knew, microwave.

See the thing is this, being single especially after a breakup is the right thing to do. Trust me. It may be hard and challenging at times but believe you me to work on yourself and develop more is much better than to be in constant pain or to cause another pain.

If we all carried on like that in this world, I think we will all be singing some 'The Black Eyed Peas – Where is the LOVE?'[6]

LESSON

By choosing to wait for your oven baked guy/lady that has gone through his or her challenges and come out fresh and fully healed is better than choosing your microwavable guy/lady that still is able or in the position to hurt or cause you pain, consciously and unconsciously, as they have not fully healed or developed themselves.

So I guess for me, I choose to wait for a non-rushed, oven baked kind of guy/relationship.

What do you choose?

---

[6]. The Black Eyed Peas - Released in June (2003) - Album: Elephunk - song written by George Pajon Jr. / Justin Timberlake / Michael Fratantuno / Printz Board / Allan Pineda / Will Adams / Jaime Gomez

3.3 Seasons

Who loves going on a roller-coaster? You queue up for a long time, you wait patiently for it to be your turn, you take your seat and finally your seat and seat belt is checked for safety measures of course and off you go.....

Slowly, slowly, the build-up comes midway through the ride and then whoosh, the peak of the ride sets in, your reaction, hysterical. Well in my case it's normally a big scream, a tight squeeze of my stomach and my eyes closed tightly whilst at times trying to take a peek. Chicken? Oh no, not at all. Ha.

It's a crazy feeling but fun at times.

Your response once the ride concludes as you make your way back to the place it all started with an exit sign rather than a welcome sign is between two to three reactions: 1) A big expression of words such as 'that was awesome', 2) A sign of relief as you share the not ever again expression on your face, or 3) I feel sick. Which I am proud to say I have not ever had response 3 happen to me, thank God. And for those who have, please do not do that to yourself again, please don't.

Singleness can be seen as having its own type of rollercoaster experience, have you noticed? For me, there are times when I am so high on being single. I am content, enjoying my friends and family and going out, not having a huge care in the world....screaming within 'I am liberated'.

If and when people ask about my single status, I respond boldly with a strong 'nope, still single, it's cool though as I am still living and breathing'…woo hoo. All high energy.

This I would like to call the 'UPSEASON'.

Then a couple of months roll over, days turn into night, new romantic movies come out, as you'll be able to know by now that I am a lover of them, so I of course go and watch them.
The pulling away from some friends especially the ones that are already couples that start to make you wish you were in a relationship begins. My response then changes to 'one day' with a sprinkle of hope in my heart.

This I would like to call the 'MIDSEASON'.

Out of nowhere, your best friend gives you the news that your ex is engaged and due to be married next month.
Your sister's boyfriend finally proposes and Jane your friend is now pregnant.
Anything else? Sure Hannah, is getting married and would like for you to be one of her bridesmaids, let the planning begin.
At this point, you're overwhelmed with all the good news that should make you smile from ear to ear, but deep down inside, you sink.

But, why? Because it is not you, nothing has drastically changed or is changing for you especially not when it comes to your single status. Go figure.
You then start to compare yourself to others and begin to think negatively rather than positively as when you used to in your up or mid-season.
This I would like to call the 'DOWN SEASON'.

The thing is at some point if we could always stay in the up season in our single lives wouldn't that be great? But as we all know and we can collectively agree, when situation tries to tell you otherwise it doesn't always happen that way, because life becomes life and things change constantly. It is for our perspective to be adjusted correctly.

I used to live in the mid/down season a lot. Never really understood friends that were in the 'up season' all the time as I thought they were just deceiving themselves.

But then what I realised is that they were not deceiving themselves, but I somewhat was.
You see in the wallowing of my 'down season' I would or let's say could miss my dear loved ones transitioning from singleness or having an amazing opportunity to be a mother or father.
I was making myself see the ashes instead of the beauty, the soil instead of the beautiful bloomed flower or the branches instead of the main tall outstanding tree.

With all this being said, we need to get to a point where we own our seasons and not allow our seasons to own us.

Being in the 'DOWN SEASON' will only steal our joy, peace and hope even if it is just a glimpse at first, which at times we cannot afford to lose out on.

Being in the MID SEASON shows us that we are still human wanting to be loved, not afraid of love and do still have interest or desires/dreams to be determined to always get us to the UP SEASON.

LESSON

I think it is healthy to be in the mid to up season, why? Because even though your perspectives challenges your life, emotions are not afraid to be in mid-season because you still have the hope of learning, developing to be the best support to others as others are to you, you will not lose sight of the great things to come.

So my advice is this: embrace your seasons as long as it's mid or up seasons. Don't let your season e.g.: Down season, push you so far down into the wrong way or a pit that you cannot get out off, because as at this point if so low, things can become a real struggle.
Each season of life especially through singleness is to be seen as a stepping stone to being stronger, wiser and determined to stay standing with your head lifted up.

I once heard a friend say, 'singleness is not a prison', so don't allow it to lock you up and the 'key' to be thrown away preventing you from doing all the amazing things you can freely do, whilst saying no to limitations.

Better yet, how about this: *"Just because we experience an emotional response (in our lives and reactions) doesn't mean that we have to act upon those emotions."* (Partially paraphrased) Nicely said by Amanda in her book 'Purify Your Life'[7]:

---

[7]. Purify Your Life by Amanda Guiseppi (2018)

As I said it before and say it again now, I dare you to own your season and don't let your season own you.

2nd Stop: Humble Avenue

3.4 Rejection

I would always say to myself and others that I cannot force someone to like me let alone love me, but that didn't take away from the FACT that I still wanted to be liked or better yet loved.

The English Oxford Living Dictionaries defines <u>rejection</u> like this,

rejection:
NOUN
mass noun

1. The dismissing or refusing of a proposal, idea, etc.
'the Union decided last night to recommend rejection of the offer'

'the rejection of the application for parole'

1.1. The action of spurning a person's affections.

'some people are reluctant to try it, because they fear rejection'

The number of times I have felt rejected or have been dealt the rejection card has been unreal. Maybe, it's because as soon as I see someone I am interested in, I make the first move and express my interest. Desperate? On reflection, yes but still hard to admit that I was desperate or that my initial move may be interpreted as desperation.

You see at the time, I always longed to be in a relationship, why? I wanted to share my life with someone, raise beautiful children together, serve and share, to be seen as someone's companion and more.
Wishful thinking!

I don't know, it's crazy when you read about what rejection is and compare it against your own life experiences, it can become rather overwhelming and actually make you completely step out of the 'denial' mindset as we may have been within and realise 'oh my, I have been given a 'NO', rejection has appeared, deep right?.

No wonder I felt unloved when I searched for 'real' love from my parents or siblings but felt I never received it much. No wonder I felt like an outcast or not good enough when I went into relationships and at times felt disrespected or mistreated. I mean wasn't I a good person in general?

Rejection can feel as cruel as a door being slammed right in your face and then what? How do you feel right at that moment? Angry, hurt, sad, worthless? I mean, rejection doesn't even take into consideration whether you are a good person or not.
Part of me feels like its right to feel how you felt right in that moment of rejection especially when your intention at the time was good. However, not to dwell in that negative place and for sure wake-up and move on.

Someone's 'no' instead of a 'yes' can come across as a very harmful word, but at the same time, I have now started to realise that as crazy as it sounds, their rejection was not God's denial in providing me with true love, hope, and a positive present and future. (Jeremiah 29:11)
Who knows where certain 'yes's' could have led to especially if within the wrong content or mindset.

I guess we should be thankful because when I think about it I am better now than I was before. I am stronger, confident, constantly growing and learning, wiser, I am myself, I know my worth and do not in any way tolerate any forms of disrespect or mistreatment, most of the things 'Faith' 11 years ago would have probably denied.

For even as a seed (planted), buried into the ground has its own setback, delay or battle with the weather seasons and more, however, the seed comes back, stronger, bigger and better when it forms into that plant, flower or even a tree.

Our attention/intention may always be good when we go after what we want in a relationship or what we strive to be, however, the intention of others might be the exact opposite.

Every time I reached out to a guy, I honestly didn't want to seem desperate, after all, one of my brothers used to send me a wake-up warning by saying: *"Faith a guy can smell desperation from afar"*, Yi,Yi,Yi.

But then please tell me, how then can a lady show interest without coming across as being desperate and receiving the rejection card without being given the opportunity to show her true lovely colours? The same with a guy, how is he meant to come across as being the supportive, strong, caring man if all he receives is negative criticism or the polite 'no'?

I remember when I joined a Christian based dating site in June 2018. It was my first attempt in a while of getting back 'with it', it had the swipe to the left if you do not like a person and swipe to the right if you do like a person kind of system going on. When I was showing the app to two of my friends, one of them said this to me: *"Faith, I hope you are not determining your worth on whether people accept you based on the swipes of 'likes' right?"* I responded with a, *"No, I know"*. And funny enough at the time, I was not 'matched' with anyone as yet, though I registered with the dating site in June 2018, I felt it was very easy to fall into the trap of weighing my worth based on the 'none' matches. But yet again, this is why I love the people I have around me (it is always vital to have good honest folks around you that genuinely care) as they always give me good checkpoints to make sure I do not lose sight of my worth or who God says I am.

Since then round about November 2018 so, about (6 months after) I registered I decided that I wanted to delete the app, why? Because, not only did my friend give me a well needed food for thought , but , to be honest, I actually would prefer to meet someone the 'old school way', i.e.: in person, despite the 'expression' that I hear of it being 'hard' to do so these days, but that's just me!

LESSON

Just because you may not get the swipes that can connect you to your potential wife or husband like others may have had, doesn't take away from how priceless, beautiful or handsome you are.

The struggle is real, trust me, I know.

To conclude this chapter, let's put it this way, as I mentioned above, I now see rejection as God's way of putting me on the right track. Giving me some backbone and helping me to see what I didn't need versus what I thought I did need.

It's like feeling as refreshed as when I listen to the song 'Take me to the King' sang by Tamela Mann[8]… It is so real and raw, honestly speaking, it almost says what I had been thinking or feeling for a very long time; as it speaks of rejection, pain, feeling, alone, empty, needing God to heal and help me (us) feel and be better.

Sometimes it's for us to also look at ourselves and ask how many times we also have rejected others, and in doing so, unintentionally and without realising ourselves the damage or hurt we may have caused others too, let alone how we may feel when it happens to us. This is not meant to make us feel bad, but it is to allow us to think about it, not just how we handle rejection, but also how we may have to gently let someone down. It is not really easy thinking about it in that way is it? But it's the truth.

You see, at times rejection wants us to scream worthless, anger, depression, guilt, pity party and more, but it's for us ladies and gents to not allow rejection to have such control over us too.

Yes, we may have received a 'no' when we really wanted a 'yes', but look on the bright side, do you know how amazing you are, it ends up being their LOSS, not yours!

Think about it this way, another's No can be another's Yes.

---

[8]. Take Me to the King, lead single from Mann's third studio album, Best Days. Label - Tillymann Music Group - Songwriter Kirk Franklin Producer(s) Kirk Franklin and Shaun Martin (2012)

CHAPTER 4

STAND STILL

4. Waiting Patiently

For the longest time, I wanted to drive my own car, which meant that I had to pass all my tests, both theory and practice.

This was a huge challenge for me because without putting in the work I could easily fail, which was the results of my first theory test.

Head down, the feeling of disappointment crept in and the sigh with the thoughts that followed as I sat on the train journey home from Watford (UK) was this: 'Here we go again, when will I ever pass this test and when will it be my turn?' sound familiar?

I constantly viewed others and where they were in life as some life goals I also needed to make.

I viewed those younger than me that passed their test or got married, creating more thoughts about who I was, where I was in my stage of life and my weaknesses and more.

Round of applause I could hear, going out especially to me because at this point I was allowing failure to embrace me, I felt like I was not moving anywhere or achieving anything, the pity party parade had begun.

All this over a driving test? Come on.

Wrong!

You see it was way more than that, that was just me giving you a taste of what the attitude of failure can do when in the midst of waiting.

We can all agree that singleness has its own waiting period as well. As you wait have you noticed that time does not wait around for you? Others status does not be put on hold because yours has and especially in the women cause, we all know our biological clock keeps on ticking away.

Now, just to pause here, regarding your biological clock ladies in my experience, this never really fazed me and really and truly, in my opinion, it should not faze you too, why? Because it shouldn't be anything you should want to stress over or dwell upon, and this is not me trying to be insensitive at all.

Check this out, I always believed that the same God who created me will bless me and my husband with children at the right time whether at this current age or older.

I used to dislike at times bumping into my old school friends with their children because as much as it was nice to see them after some time the 'norm' conversation arises regarding, marriage and have you any of your own type of questions… even though my response was always polite, it always used to dawn on me that so many of them already had children and I didn't. It took me a few conversations like this to realise, it was okay and that one day I will have my own.

There may be some of you like one of my friends that do not want children, as well as some of you who feel they would like to adopt (such a beautiful thing), with this being said, your biological clock will continue to tick away, but that does not mean that God is not faithful and that he will not bless you, as through others testimonies even in an older age, healthy childbirth has still been possible, so there remains hope, especially for those of you that really want children.

So, let me give you a Biblical reference: Genesis 17:17 *"Abraham fell facedown; he laughed and said to himself, "Will a son be born to a man a hundred years old? Will Sarah bear a child at the age of ninety?"*

Genesis 21:2 *"Sarah became pregnant and bore a son to Abraham in his old age, at the very time God had promised him."*

As we can see, Abraham laughed at this thought even in the Biblical times when God truly was manifesting himself and there maybe some of you who are doing the same, thinking many things you wish and hoped for is impossible.

But as we see in Matthew 19:26 *"With men this is impossible, but with God all things are possible."* And with this being said, if we follow Abraham and Sarah's story to the end, we could see that God remained faithful to His word and also to His promises.

I guess the point I am making here before we move on from this is: A healthy home, a stable family with love and care and a solid Christ grounding is an environment I would love to raise my children. In my mind I would love to be a mother and my husband-to-be, to be an amazing father to our children, but for the sake of waiting, be it however long, I refused to be pregnant to the wrong person out of fear that my biological clock was ticking away; providing my children with a great foundation is more important to me.

I truly, truly applaud all single parents, especially those that tried to build a solid, healthy, loving family foundation for their children, but it didn't work out with the person you thought it would. I salute your dedication to your children and want you to know that you are a great mother or father and don't ever stop hoping and believing that your spouse will come if you desire it.

But, if the above is not your story and yours is similar to mines, choose to wait. Close your legs to be in a better relationship, where there is genuine respect, love, selflessness and more great things, it is possible, where not only you will benefit but also your spouse and children will too.

Even if we wanted to speed up this process, which I know we possibly could without boasting, let it not be an option for us where our standards are dropped. If I wasn't bothered to wait and just settled I know I would 100% end up with the microwavable relationship/man rather than the real oven-baked relationship/man as mentioned in Chapter 3:2 that I had always wanted.

Let's not kid ourselves or fall short of the blessings we can receive for the lack of waiting in our single season.

As we wait for the bus, train or plane to get us to our destinations, it's the same feeling as waiting on our spouse to appear, to be a mother or father to go on dates and much more.

I think if there was an easy way to wait I am sure by now we will have all taken that route a long time ago and claimed our awards for 'hanging in there', but as reality shows us every day, each individuals waiting period is different, but with patience, endurance, we learn, may make mistakes along the way, but will grow rather than be ignorant to not learn anything at all.

One thing that keeps creeping up also in conversation with married or dating couples is the question raised before of interested in anyone? Even when you say no, their response would normally be, do not worry I am sure he is coming....But even as that conversation concludes, it dawned on me, what else could they have said?

The above is just to show that as singles, you need to be prepared for whatever question, debate or doubt may come your way through your waiting period, and especially in your thoughts you need to know how to handle peer pressure and conversations like the above from known and unknown individuals and notice that waiting reveals a lot, starting with who your real supporters are, your true friends, 'enemies' or even those who do not have time for you.

I know for me and some of my other friends and family, this waiting period has been one of the hardest parts of our single journeys, not even facing being abstinence or knowing you don't want to settle, especially as previously mentioned when you see everyone else's dream/s coming true.

You always hear about waiting for the right time for your spouse to come, but do not forget to have patience whilst doing so. How hard can this be?

At the first stages of my single journey, patience was not ever my strongest point. I must confess I do like things in a particular 'proper' way at a particular time, sometimes, okay, maybe all the time. (ha), but doesn't it seem like your patience is always being tested, especially when it involves others? Selfish as I know as this may sound. But hey that's how I felt.

Having patience I once read in Joyce Meyer's devotional book, said this: *"...patience is more than the ability to wait, it's is the ability to keep a GOOD ATTITUDE while waiting."* [9] Very interesting right?
Well, my attitude was not in a good place whilst trying to be patient in waiting, so clearly at the time; I did not take Joyce Meyers advice.
I guess cause I was feeling unloved, missed out and in need of that hole/void to be filled quickly, patience at the time was not my friend.

---

[9] Closer to God each day devotional: God's timing is the right timing, Pg. 209

See, catch this, I said hole/void, as we all have that gap on the pursuit of happiness, breakthroughs and more but we must choose to fill that hole/void with the right things of Christ's love first and everything healthy.

If I was speaking to a guy of interest and was waiting on his response, I was that lady that if there was a few minutes or an hour, pushing it to a day late for a response to be received, that was far too long for me to wait. I needed at the time that response to be now at that moment, despite them most likely having a valid reason for their delayed response.

Being patient for me was never something I 100% mastered as I can openly admit; I am still trying to work on this even now. But I must say in learning a few tips along the way, it has enabled me to understand the process of waiting but at the same time not to jump too quickly into anything I was not meant to be in at all.
I remember when I had a faith moment and said to God. 'I don't mind if you bless everyone with their love before me, I just want to see everyone happy.'

What? Rewind, what was I thinking?

Later on in life that conversation with God started to surface with realistic results, call it a coincidence if you like, but I started to see one by one through my friends and family's life, marriages, babies and more becoming true. It then started eating me up to the point where I remembered what I said to God and I had to quickly ask for forgiveness, grace in case I was wrong to say such prayers asking that I do not be left to the end of waiting for my dreams and desires to be married to come true.

Was this me having a humbling, wake up or a selfish moment? Or could it just be me having a 'meltdown', only God knows what that was all about at the time.

I also realised that nobody really talks about this subject: WAITING. But thank God to my surprise I was so happy to see that Meagan Good and husband Devon Franklin bought out a book touching on similar subjects called 'The Wait',[10] which I do recommend you to read.

But when you really think of the silent and dry seasons in our lives and you think is anyone going to see you? Don't you realise that peer pressure cries, as well as temptation tries to call your name, settlement, loneliness screams louder with their proposal too. But then what? What becomes your response?

I remember really having to ask God if He had called me for marriage or not. I also poured out my heart in prayer to Him and said if He did not, then to take away the desires of being married and a mother so that I can be at peace and just know His will for me so that I can just continue to live life, but clearly I felt that he still kept the desire within me and here I stand still wanting to be married and to have children.

I think above all this, if there is anything that stood out to me whilst waiting was this. I know that when you pray believing for things, just make sure you know 100% what you're praying for because if the time is right you might just get it, but the question is, will you be ready? And that goes for every part of your life.

Waiting patiently doesn't mean you stop going out and having fun with your friends, ignoring the times you feel alone and expressing or filling

---

[10] The Wait: A Powerful Practice for Finding the Love of Your Life and the Life You Love by DeVon Franklin and Meagan Good – (Sept 2015)

that with spending more time with God, going on retreats, concerts, holidays with friends, family, yourself and more. Waiting patiently means to do all those things and more, not forgetting yourself, desires, hopes and dreams in the process, but allowing yourself to be free, discovering and walking in your purpose whilst being single available but not desperate.

As I tried again and studied real hard for my next driving theory and practical test I was greeted with the response that I HAD PASSED. A few months later I got my first car, lovely, and shiny blue, just right for me and there you had it, the wait was over and I now drive around everywhere.

LESSON

In these waiting seasons I learnt a lot along the way, as I retook my driving tests I went through all weather conditions (snow, rain, sunny days and more), Yes it may have taken me longer to master it all and endure such weather conditions (some better than the others), but with constant support from my instructor and family I became better.

To be able to drive with confidence, knowing that whatever weather conditions came along I was fully prepared is so much better than driving with unsurety or fear. The same goes for your single journey too. All your development, trails, mistakes, growth, healing, studies and strength will allow you to grasp your waiting stage and it can only be an insight or eye-opener because I believe that when a heart that has truly waited and depended on God whilst walking in His will, will have the results of a great marriage and your relationship will be sweet enough.

Having patience develops you over time.

I understand it may be hard at first especially when you're waiting on your answer right away. But as I can now say that I am getting better at this, I am not 100% there yet, but it doesn't mean I will quit trying to do so. I am sure you can also too. You will also realise through this change of mentality, you will face less pain, hurt and rejection.

Patience will now become your friend as it has become mine.

Being and remaining obedient to God will result in Gods blessings and opportunities to you, so take time/ make time to always be in His presence wherever you can.

Psalm 27:14 puts it this way: "Wait on the Lord: be of good courage, and he shall strengthen thine heart: wait, I say, on the Lord."

So as we pray and hope, we wait with great expectation, embracing this single journey patiently believing and hoping that one day God will hear us and that our wait to be married will soon be over.

CHAPTER 5

STANDING ALONE

5. A.L.O.N.E?

Feeling alone is not a nice feeling at all.

As you watch happy families in front of you, couples walking hand in hand or sharing a kiss on the street, it's almost like an automatic trigger is set off in you and your thoughts go instantly to your emotions and you say those five words: " I wish that was me, followed with another three words: 'I feel alone'. Mannnnnn.

The reality for me was that I was not ever really alone, I had The Holy Spirit who is constantly with me and you too **(Please read Psalm 139: 7-10 and John 14:15-31**). That of course is if you know him through salvation having the Christian Biblical foundation: John 3:16-17 *"For God so loved the world that he gave his one and only Son, that whoever believes in him shall not perish but have eternal life. For God did not send his Son into the world to condemn the world, but to save the world through him."*

Even though I had a strong network of friends and family around me too, and the vague knowledge at the time that yes somebody one day would want and accept me, in saying that, I still felt alone and this reality came after 3-4 years from now.

After my breakup with my ex-boyfriend/fiancé (which was the longest relationship I had ever been in) being alone felt like a constant battle which I felt at the time I couldn't win.

There were times when I felt worthless and weak to the point where I would beat myself up for being such a nice person inside….well at least that's what I thought at the time, nice people always get mistreated….wrong.

I was once told: *"Faith, don't ever change who you are because you gave your love to someone and they did not cherish it"*. (Paraphrased).

But that was the point right there. After giving the person I thought was the 'right' person for me, my genuine love and care; the 'right' person become the 'wrong' person, who then I felt at the time messed up my dreams and left me standing alone. No relationship, no husband and no potential, point blank.

It was bad enough that I didn't 100% feel loved at home, no matter what my parents or siblings ever said. I felt as though all the pain of 'daring to love' and wanting to be loved and not receiving it in the way I felt at the time I needed to feel was just thrown in my face.

On reflection of how I was treated in and outside of my family, it almost made love seem like it was not real. Rejection screamed my name and I felt as if I didn't matter.

So at this point, not only was I dealt the single card, but now also the rejection and lonely card too. Not great because at this rate my cards were piling up.

I tried to carry on as 'normal' as I could, I went to functions, church, walked down the street, sat on the train, or took trips to the movies, but still felt alone.

You know that image when being in a room full of people and then the lights shine down on that one person and the camera zooms in on you only, whilst everyone else around you disappears into pitch black? Yes, that feeling…. How crazy is that right?

Que in Celine Dion song: 'All by myself, don't want to be all by myself anymore'[11]…STOP!

Have you ever heard people talk about some individuals having so many people around them, even being in relationships but yet still feel alone? How real is that? Actually, believe it or not, it's so real. There was a campaign that went on to end loneliness and the research stated that the *"impact loneliness can make on our health is that loneliness increases the likelihood of mortality by 26% and is a bigger problem than simply an emotional experience"*[12].

According to the Relate website (newsletter) *"Almost seven million UK adults* – more than 1 in 8 of us (13%) – report having no close friends**, according to research out today from leading relationships charities Relate and Relationships Scotland. This has increased from 1 in 10 (10%) when the same question was asked in 2014 and 2015.*

The charities' new report, You're not alone – the quality of the UK's social relationships, also found that almost half (45%) of UK adults say they feel lonely at least some of the time and almost a fifth (18%) said that they feel lonely often or all of the time. Sadly, almost one in six (17%) said they never (5%) or rarely (12%) feel loved.[13]"

---

[11] Celine Dion song: All by myself - Songwriters: Eric Carmen / Sergei Rachmaninoff – (1996)

[12] https://www.campaigntoendloneliness.org/loneliness-research/ (2018)

[13] https://www.relate.org.uk/about-us/media-centre/press-releases/2017/2/22/loneliness-rising-1-8-adults-have-no-close-friends (Release date: March 2017)

This is just to show that loneliness is real and very present in our world today, more than we think it is, what is the cause for the stats above? We may not 100% know, due to everyone's personal feelings and experiences. However, after listening to a discussion about this on the radio whilst coming home from work as well as reading these different articles, a few times it was mentioned individual's reasons were because they felt abandoned, alone in marriages, being stuck within their own thoughts, comparison and much more. Therefore, I think it best that we really try to avoid any feelings of being alone wherever we best can.

When it comes to singleness and marriage, many individuals would like to quote Genesis 2:18 *"It is not good for the man to be alone. I will make a helper suitable for him."* Not that it isn't right to do so, but I believe it also suggests that as humans living on this earth we all need somebody as family, friend, love (companion) and more, do you agree?

I also think it's all to do with our mindset. If you are blinded by your hurt and pain as I was, you will not be able to see or feel real love or acceptance from anybody and especially from God, unless you allow yourself to HEAL; meaning, you allow God in to help you forgive others of any wrongs they have done to you. Forgiving yourself of any wrongs you have done to yourself and others, as well as know deep down as much as we all long to be loved by another it doesn't mean we need that significate others to feel 'complete', rather we should feel complete in God and ourselves even before that man or lady comes into our lives.

Therefore in renewing our minds *"Don't copy the behavior and customs of this world, but let God transform you into a new person by changing the way you think. Then you will learn to know God's will for you, which is good and pleasing and perfect."* Romans 12:2 NLT, we no longer feel lonely due to not feeling accepted by everyone in the world or meeting up to their standards instead at this point we should now feel accepted by our friends, family and especially by God.

We allow ourselves to HEAL and realise we may not be perfect and always have everything together, but we are on the way to being the BEST version of ourselves for any situation we may find ourselves in, filling our loneliness with things that make us feel loved.

Please, don't believe that nobody understands your current position of being single and feeling lonely, because we all do, we know how it feels and what you're experiencing and know it's not a nice feeling at all at times, so try not to cut out the people who truly love you and want to be there for you.

I know personally I can be guilty of this, because at times I tend to reserve how I feel, not allowing anyone in to help, where I then tend to block everyone else out, but then only to realise that it is not fair on those around me who really is concerned and cares.

At times I also understood that you just have to face your loneliness and see that it's not a way of God trying to punish you. But for you to demand that it does not control you and that's exactly what I had to do.

By turning this alone feelings of emotions to work for me rather than against me, was one of the best decisions I could have made on my single journey.

Being and feeling alone can be a very secluded place and it's not a place that we should get comfortable in to make it our home, not now and not ever.

Yes, there are times when I love being in my own personal space, no one to answer to or disturb me etc. I remember Joyce Meyer, once saying it this way: *"Alone doesn't always mean loneliness"*, which is so true.

However, I personally had to make a choice to not be stuck in a rut feeling so sorry for myself or my situation, and thinking that to be happy and fulfilled I needed to be in a relationship, or have things, noooooo, as much as all those things are great and would be nice, I needed to get out more, enjoy my life with my genuine friends and family, enjoy their company and begin to see myself for the person I really was, beautiful, having great people around me and not alone.

I love how Megan Good said it in 'The Wait': 'God doesn't show your heart to everybody. He only shows it to people He can trust with it' (Xiv).[14] How awesome are those simple but profound words?

Breakups in relationships/friendships and even with family can always make you feel alone especially when time, emotions, energy and more have been invested. But in the midst of that there's a comforting voice that reassures us by saying this: *'Though your father and mother (brother, sister, friends etc.) forsake (abandon) you the Lord will (hold/take you) receive you'* Psalm 27:10 (paraphrased).

After reading this verse understanding the depth of his promise to me, I realised that God made me feel accepted and not alone reminding me of His true LOVE (John 3:16). I then started to see the real LOVE I was missing through my genuine friends that always stood by me even when I made mistakes and my family who really cared and made time for me where they could. Finally, I made the right choice and that was to see their love and my love for myself.

Carrying fewer mistakes, self-pity and baggage, and choosing to move forward with support, whilst not allowing yourself to be isolated, you really find out that you truly are not alone. So get connected positively

---

[14.] The Wait: A Powerful Practice for Finding the Love of Your Life and the Life You Love Book by DeVon Franklin and Meagan Good (2015)

where you need to. Join a small group at church or laugh a bit with your school friends, colleagues and family. Make the time to spend with real down to earth friends and let friendship blossom in all the places they need to.

Today I know that I can go to the movies by myself and enjoy my own company. I remember hearing Heather Lindsay,[15] once say the same thing as how she used to go on date nights with God. So sweet and so cool, I do the same to the movies especially at those times when the lonely thoughts try to come to mind and there is no one else able to go out with. You are an overcomer, so believe it.

LESSON

Remember you got to tell yourself that 'you got this'. Don't worry about feeling alone at times, it's natural because your heart wants to love and be loved. How many married couples especially the ones with children, even though they love their families still at times long for 'alone time'.

See, let's not rush to be where they are, missing the gems in this single season of alone time here because whatever happens next, we do not want to regret anything or miss out on what valued lessons our single lives was trying to tell us when we thought we were feeling alone.

'Singleness is not isolation, singleness is restoration and clarification.'

---

[15] Founder of Pinky Promise and a Christian author

It is also good to know that when we accept Jesus into our hearts and become followers of Christ we become a family, we become a part of His family, check what Ephesians 2:19 says: "you are no longer foreigners and strangers, but fellow citizens with God's people and also members of his household" where we stand as brothers and sisters in Him helping to share with each other's burdens, defeating the isolation notion and clinging onto the truth that we have the best support we can ever imagine to have.

(If you would like to join this amazing family, please read the SALVATION PRAYER in the appendix section under this chapter number).

On that note, take a listen to this song by Kari Jobe[16] called: 'I am not alone', it's such a beautiful song, with such beautiful and meaningful words.

3rd Stop: Chill Street

[16.] Kari Brooke Jobe is an American contemporary Christian music singer and songwriter. Songwriters: Austin Davis / Ben Davis / Dustin Sauder / Grant Pittman / Kari Jobe / Marty Sampson / Mia Fieldes

CHAPTER 6

BAGGAGE

6. Leave the past in the past

Baggage. Some heavy some light, which are you carrying and what does your bag contain? Did you pack it yourself or did someone help you?

Security clearance not checked.

You normally hear such questioning at the airport, why? So that the airline knows you're not going to cause yourself and others harm. It's their rules and what they say goes.

For me, my baggage was self-pity, a nasty breakup that left me broken, in pain, feeling ill-treated, depressed, self-consciousness, fearful, shameful and more. You name it and I packed it.

Some I must admit was packed by others on my journey of life, whereas I realised I personally packed the rest, by allowing my mind to believe the lies or even entertain the negative thoughts of others around me.

I never really realised that I had baggage until I was talking about my relationship experiences to my cousin who then responded by saying: *"Faith, you really need to free yourself and let go of your baggage (pain, hurt etc.) because it will not be nice nor fair on the next person that comes along to deal with"* (paraphrased) and in all honesty....SHE WAS 100% RIGHT.

I had carried so much pain and ache and felt a huge amount of betrayal when I found out that I was cheated on and more. I don't think anyone would want such news especially after all the investment you had placed in that relationship, as for me it slightly made me feel like I was not good enough or just enough in general. If it wasn't for people that loved me, telling me it's not true and don't believe the 'hype' I would have been worse off than how I was at the time.

I had dealt with the pain of verbal abuse in which you had to be careful it didn't run your life as it tried to do mines, as well as realising how much weight it was building up in my life baggage that now my luggage that was okay in weight became overweight.

With that being said in the real world, you would have to PAY extra to carry that type of baggage around or get RID of a few things; the consequence of the weight begins to stare you in the face. So then, what do you choose to do?

Guess what I CHOSE, I chose to get rid of the unnecessary weight.

Right now, you may feel like you either have way more baggage than me to the point that you have excess baggage and you may need to pay the extra cost or you may be in the other line where you have less. Whichever line you stand in, you need to realise that releasing all baggage gives you the FREEDOM to walk with no heavy burden and you're not held back.

Baggage's for me are things of your past and sometimes your present especially things that can prevent you from living and moving forward in your single world and life in general that could stop you from reaching your married world. It would be far more painful and consequential to be married and carry baggage into something that is new; for this reason marriage with baggage that was not sorted out suffers and no healing takes place, in some cases this might lead to divorce.

For me, personally I wouldn't want to carry baggage throughout my single life, and then into marriage, hurting myself, my spouse and even our children, I would rather take the time now to get rid of my baggage.

How about you?

But, if that is you (speaking to married folks now), it's not too late, work on your marriage and start from now, get rid of unnecessary baggage in your life and be free in your marriage to truly LOVE again, you'll see it will make a huge difference, but you need to be willing and truly communicate how you feel.

One of those well-known sayings comes to mind when I think of 'baggage', I've said it before, but I will quote again Will Bowen[17] where he said: *'Hurt people, hurt people'*. That cannot and should not be your story or something to carry over at all. And if this may confuse you, maybe you just need to change the way you look at your baggage's to see the real weight of the ones that you have been carrying and what those weights represent: Lost, un-forgiveness, hurt, pain, abuse, mistreatment, manipulation, self-harm and so forth?

You at least want to make sure that the next relationship you step into starts with a clean slate, not a complicated overly guarded one.

So right now, how about we get proactive again; let's explore what is in the baggage that has been weighing on you. I would like you to do something brave for me.

---

[17] Will Bowen - Motivational Speaker and Author

Take this time to really think and be honest with yourself. Write down what baggage is in your life be it big or small (heavy or light) from old to recent:

1)

2)

3)

4)

If you've done so, Well done, proud of you. (If you skipped this bit, please try, it will help you, really it would).

Next step is to write down ways in which you are going to get rid of them and overcome them.

For example:

One of mines was self-pity……. My way of overcoming this was by telling myself, this was a mistake and not totally my fault. I tried my best and it didn't work. I forgave myself, and especially the person that wronged me and wish them well, but now I must move on.

Luke 6:28 puts it this way: *"bless those who curse you, pray for those who mistreat you"*. As well as Romans 12:14 says: *"Bless those who persecute you. Don't curse them; pray that God will bless them."*

I remember as hard as it was to deal with all that I had experienced with my ex-fiancé, I had to find it somewhere in my heart to pray the prayers of forgiveness and blessings.

Praying to God that he knows Him (God) and does not mistreat the next lady as he did me etc, not missing out speaking blessings upon him and his household. Was this easy? Not at all, to be honest, it was really hard to do as at the same time when injustice or mistreatment is seen you only want justice, but was that for me to deliver? After all I was no saint too, I mean, who is?

But I had to remember what God said in His word: *"The battles are not mines but the Lord"* 2 Chronicles 20:15 so there I rested; it was all in Christ hands.

This almost becomes a 'wake up and smell the coffee' kind of moment. It's a new day type of feeling. Remember you only feel how you allow yourself to feel, so why not feel great by getting over the past pains and issues.

Your Turn…Go:

1)

2)

3)

4)

Doing this writing exercise should show you that having baggage and being able to identify it enables you to show yourself and others (if it matters) that you are willing to leave the past (whatever time frame that could be) there and that you are determined to heal and move forward.

Holding on to unnecessary baggage just doesn't do you any good, neither makes any sense.

There will be some people (fake people) that are not in support of your healing process and could easily say that they cannot see you changing or healing, and constantly like to drag up the pass, don't let them.

Like me, I had to prove them wrong, not just to show them, but to prove to myself most of all, that I can do it, enough was enough I became free to love and be loved again, because I knew that I didn't want any type of baggage weighing or distracting me from my happy ever after, in whatever capacity that could be.

LESSON

After some years, let's say 11 years went by, I then received a message.
It was my Ex.
Say what!
Yep, are you as baffled as I was?
I actually thought it was a joke until I continued to read his message.

To keep it brief and respectful, he basically said sorry. Asked for forgiveness and admitted to not treating me right and for me to know that I was worth being with and that he appreciated all that I did. Whilst wishing me the best respectfully.

Gulp!
This truly blew my mind.

I responded, to let him know that I had already forgiven him a long time ago and that he should feel 'free' from any guilt.

He couldn't believe it himself especially after reflecting knowing of all that he had put me through; but to be honest that was that. We continued to speak as if nothing 'crazy' had happened between us. But then I knew deep down it had to be cut short in respect to him moving on with his family and I not trying to rekindle what was completed in the past.

I was healed and was not looking to 'unheal' and I could only hope that he knew I didn't hate him at all but really appreciated the fact that he came to say sorry.

This example is just to show that SORRY can heal. Choosing to say no to hurt and pain, whilst forgiving others who I must add is not perfect too, makes all the difference.

I believe if I didn't ask God to heal and help me through the pains I felt from my past relationship, I may have responded differently if I had read his response then.

So thank God I did. God's grace is truly so sufficient for each and every one of us, check out how Paul puts it in 2 Corinthians 12:9 *"My grace is sufficient for you, for my power is made perfect in weakness. Therefore I will boast all the more gladly about my weaknesses, so that Christ's power may rest on me",* I don't think we realise how much so.

So please do choose to let the past go, truly forgive were you need to and begin to get excited about your present leading to your future.

4th Stop: Freedom Road

CHAPTER 7

OTHERS PERSPECTIVES

7. What do others & YOU see?

"It's you and your cousin left now" was a statement my mum made to me as we were talking with each other.

I actually don't think she meant anything unkind or harmful about what she said when she said it, in fact, she was just stating a slight fact which had an element of truth to it as we were talking about one of my other cousin's engagement.

Whether you go to weddings, events or hear of another engagement, the question of being single or dating anyone will always or let's say 85% of the time come up as mentioned before.

I even remembered one of my friends who was highly annoyed and down about this whole singles journey, she wasn't impressed with the questioning as I wasn't too. Especially when being asked by 'the aunties and uncles' at family and friend's weddings the same questions: "When is it going to be your turn?" i.e.: When are you going to get married? Almost like they are instantly expecting you to give a full blown date, time, location and more. Huh?

For me, when now asked I normally like to throw in the response: 'Ask God', which tends to stop them from asking further.

I remember having to tell my same friend not to worry about such questions because if she did it can easily force her to be in a relationship that she shouldn't be in for the sake of silencing the questions of others. Yi,Yi,Yi.

My same friend mentioned that it even got to a point where she felt so pressured that not only did frustration with the whole singleness come in, but also a slight call of desperation too.

If only her handsome man would just come along now to swoop her away and silence all the chats, questions and speculators that would have been great, but that wasn't her current reality.

As much as others may wish you well, and ask you the 'questions' innocently, some may not realise nor understand that in your single journey it's just not that simple at times. And because of that, you tend to say the wrong thing at the wrong time, which can birth ideas, suggestions or even feelings that you have been trying to fight off all your single life.

It must be hard on our parents too I guess, especially when they attend their friends children's weddings and are also questioned as to their own children. I get it, it's tough on them too, and I see this especially when I speak to my mum about upcoming weddings, as much as she is happy for them, her reactions say it clearer as she reflects on her own children who are not yet married.

I think it is fair to say that some friends and family should be a little more cautious or sensitive to the single woman or man's hearts before they ask the questions, especially when that single individual is trying to make things work in a non-forceful way.

It's not like we don't want to hear good things or the obvious stated, but I guess there is just the 'right time' for it. Don't get me wrong there are some perspectives worth thinking over, let's say a specific reason that will encourage you and build you up, you know your girls or guys that are plainly looking out for you. That's why it's good to be able to use wisdom in filtering the negative perspectives so that you can see the positive ones instead.

On a side note: recently a conversation sparked up and it was relating to me writing this book as well as how a popular Morning TV program in the UK was exploring whether it was possible to find love at 50 plus. Now for me in particular, when asked what my thoughts on this were, this is what I said: **"LOVE HAS NO AGE",** with additionally saying, when love finds you, it just finds you.

Even though singleness can catch anybody, both the young and the old I believe so can love too. I've heard and seen successful love stories ending in healthy relationships and even marriages of those over 40 and upwards including not missing out on the miracles and great news of still having children too despite the ticking biological clock as mentioned in chapter 4. In my personal opinion, yes I understand there are those who choose not to be in a relationship and stay single, but as you know within this book it's all about those who do want a relationship, so on that note I also know that many want to be loved too, so, therefore, it shouldn't really be a discussion as to whether it is still possible for 40/50 years and older to still want to long for love or find love as no matter what your age, you can want love in all its galore.

It's also so important to personally know where you stand within yourself and not give in to peer pressure, especially from those dear to you, because if you are not careful you will end up dating the wrong person for the sake of dating.

Sometimes I like to think of it this way: You have well wishes for me and just want me to date someone, get married and move on....but it's not that simple because once all the vows are said, celebrations, cutting the cake, eating good food and dancing is all over, YOU will remain the one left with that person, his or her personality and not the one who is pressuring you to get into a relationship.

LESSON

In all honesty, I would rather be with someone I truly love, cherish, admire, respect and more, than to be with someone who may seem good on paper, but I don't even like for the sake of pleasing others!

And in the simplest way of saying the above: Thanks but no thanks.

5th Stop: What you saying avenue

CHAPTER 8

WHAT DO MEN AND WOMEN REALLY THINK?

8. Just a few of us

He said, she said, we all said.

In this chapter, I would like us to see how women and men feel about being single, and see each other from both a married and non-married perspective.

I grew up with three brothers and one sister, so technically I would say I have been schooled in knowing lots about how guys are etc., well so I thought. The amazing thing I realised is that in life, in general, you can never know enough, there is always something to learn and especially when it comes to the opposite sex, we are similar but different at the same time.

A couple of my friends got together and answered these two main questions:

IF MARRIED	1.	What did singleness mean to you before you were married?
	2.	What was your perspective/view of women/men?
IF SINGLE/DATING	1.	What does singleness mean to you?
	2.	What is your perspective/view of men/women?

Here are their responses: *(to view without spelling errors or slang, do see the appendix)*

KEYS: (MMR) – Married Man Response (SWR|SMR) – Single Women's/Man's Response (DMR) – Dating Man's response

	Question 1	**Question 2**
MMR	Singles in the context of that via a relationship meant the freedom to do whatever I wanted with whomever I wanted (if I could get some attention from someone ha-ha). It meant I could live life without the complications of an emotional rollercoaster playing havoc within. I meant that my pocket wasn't regularly emptying on dates and meals and other things couples do. It meant I could just go cinema or out for a meal with friends or anything social alone and I wouldn't be expected to have to pick up or drop off any bae. I was responsible to myself only. It meant I didn't have to text/WhatsApp that one person and invest my time in that one person. On one hand it meant that I wasn't burdened with the physical expectations of certain relationships that could cause me to compromise my faith. Though	At the time girls were hungry for great guys, and I could play the game like a professional. They need what they wanted but many times they irritated me cos they wanted a certain type of man. The good looking earner, the philanthropist, the Godly guy who still had a bit of thug in him and respected women. But 99% of girls I knew at the time weren't ready for such a guy. Many wanted the guy they saw in reality TV shows and Disney movies and ones that were on the outside great boyfriends/husband's, but they were not ready to compromise and settle for the friend who was everything their dream guy was to be and more. The older I got/get the funnier the situation got..those cool friend zoned guys who used to fall back and let the Disney bf/husband shine they started to settle down with girls who were quick to recognise the potential and

	I was still conscious that I had to be careful not become a promiscuous hypocrite lol cos it's wayyy too easy to invest any time I choose in something temporary and carnal. Every now and then at a wedding or a social function there was a wistful thought that I wished I was with someone meaningful cos it meant companionship and friendship and as I got older it meant settling down.	those who might have been a little more choosy or just wanted to play about and not be fixing up and getting their lives together were starting to get a little less choosy..not in a bad way..but in a way where they realise now that good boy next door is now a man of God and has married the thugged out Godly Hustlers might not be around anymore or he picked one of the thirty girls who chased him lol.. I laugh when they say that there are wayyy more girls to guy ratio..but I feel like for all the multitude of Godly, hot Hustlers girls out there..only a select few are ready for a real relationship...the Rest are still on their journey.
MMR	Well when I was single I was in the world, so I guess as a boy/man it is usually about impressing women, some guys actually said that all of life is about women so they will do everything to get women. There are different classes of guys, some who don't care about impressing women (gangsters and players) some who live for impressing women (sweet boys) and some who find it hard to get women. So depending of what kind you are your perspective	Ok now, I try to see women as sisters and human beings, before my mind was clouded with a false view of a woman worth, as mentioned above. As I have sisters I possibly found it easier to have genuine relationships with women as friends. So in a nut shell woman are literally humans like myself but made for a different purpose. I dare not glorify woman or look down on them, I see them as human and Gods daughters.

	of women would be different. I had a bit of all of them depending on the time of my life, I guess I started off in the don't care place because I was, then sweet boy, then hard to get then back to don't care, so it really depended on my mind frame at a particular time. Girls are often seen as objects because men are visually stimulated by women (women also by men) so that they see women as trophies they can get, I.e. in music videos women are portrayed to be assets.. I have more just at work	
SWR	It is a season where I find out what I truly want in a partner and also allowing me to grow as a woman and prepare for my partner.	Men need to make moves...be open with their interest...lead...pursue etc. Yeah defo all of that.. Largely the guy should be the approacher.. But I know nowadays it's not always like that, which is fine too. But I do think it's traditionally a 'man's role' to hunt for the girl (if that makes sense lol).
SWR	Singleness means to me a season of devotion. I get to be devoted completely to Jesus because I have no other responsibilities. It's a time of action. I get to be Jesus' hands and feet all over. It's a time of	That's an interesting one. I feel that single guys are wanting to get married, but they aren't willing to do the hard work that it takes to make themselves ready for marriage. A season of singleness for men

	growth. I can focus solely on growing myself to make me ready all works from the Master.	should be marked by devotion to God. When they are so devoted to God their will align with God's will for their lives and their eyes will be open to who their wife will be. A lot of single guys I met aren't that devoted to God and are too caught up in wanting to find a mate before they become the right mate. I hope that's what you wanted. Lol.
SMR	Singleness is freedom and loneliness. You're happy you can do as you please but sad cause u miss certain comforts...	All I can say about ladies is I try 2 show respect to all ladies as it was my single mum that raised me , so on the whole I would say strong but each person is judged on their own merit
SWR	It depends what you have been through already.. so if you've constantly been in relationships then being single u will almost feel like you're free.. u only have to consider yourself when making decisions etc. Whereas if you've been single for a long time u will probably prefer the relationship and maybe see others in relationships and think u will enjoy having that someone to do things with. So it depends where u are in your life. It can be a good or bad thing... kind of like "the grass always looks greener"	Men are like a box of chocolates, you never know what you're gonna get ☺ It's hard to say.. or make a statement about men. Everyone's different in their own way.. I don't understand most men. They should come with some sort of manual ☺ U could see a guy that looks like the perfect gentleman.. all suited up and dressed well but can be a complete nightmare.. and u could see someone in trackies who turns out to be the gentleman... but us woman will probably go for the one suited up just

	situation.	because of the look until we get to know them and realise they have to dress to impress coz their personality sucks 😄 I have noticed some guys do that.. they will have all the bling and designer crap just to impress because they can't do it any other way Not saying EVERY guy is like hat but it is something over noticed. I think men act very different depending who they are around. Like if they're with mates they can be hitting on girls etc. Trying to "act hard" but when they're alone they're completely different.... why?! Just be yourself all the time!
SMR	If you're asking what it means right now, I see being single as a bit of freedom. But that's after being in a longgggg relationship. I think it's different for you if you don't have options. If you didn't you'd defiantly feel a way about it. I'm open to getting into a relationship too. ALOT of people get hung up on age	"Don't be a hard rock when you really are a gem" - Lauren Hill The women (or perceived bitches) that act like they will eat a man alive are really soft

	etc...mainly females (body clock). As a man it's slightly different so I don't feel too much pressure. In summary I feel kind of philosophical about life in general. If it happens all good. If not, all good. Not everyone in a relationship is happy and the grass always looks greener on the other side.	
DMR	Singleness at the young age means.. Just having Fun.. Party life.. Dating with no commitments.. Being single at the old age is complicated.. Some could say its Freedom..but its Lonely as a prison cell..	What I find funny is that.. You already know the guy likes you..but you will judge him by his words n action initially.. What you don't know is that poor guy is nervous as hell..

These two questions were interesting to ask because I noticed not only did it spark curiosity, but it also sparked open debate, conversations, insights, greater understanding amongst both ladies and gents, clarity and so much more.

A change effect had taken place.

I think as much as some of the world would like to proclaim the whole quote from John Gray *'men are from mars and women are from Venus'*[18], it is fair to say that it doesn't take away from the FACT that yes we may be different in more obvious ways than some, but most importantly when it comes to singleness we are very similar. Just like both Mars and Venus are both planets (ha). Our approach in things may be different but our end

---

[18] Men Are from Mars, Women Are from Venus Author: John Gray - 1992

goal, if we have the right perspectives, is completely the same, to be loved and to give love.

LESSON

Remember, ladies and gents we are not enemies here, we need to show each other as much respect as possible and work things out together where needed rather than against each other.

Tell me something, Why cause a division where there doesn't need to be one? Why not unite instead!

In my experiences having my down to earth, real guys as my friends have helped a lot as well as having my down to earth girls too.

I do like how one of my friends said it this way, about searching for your potential partners: *"There is no such thing as PERFECT partner; you just think they are perfect cos you have lots of things in common and click so well you obviously become attracted to each other."*

We all have a perspective on singleness, there is always going to be a make or break point for us to determine whether we will be in or out of a relationship. For this reason we can all fairly agree that we are not all perfect. It's quite humbling to be able to admit that isn't it?

Getting out of being single when the time is right is being able to see two imperfect people coming together to make a 'perfect picture, beginning, middle and end'.

82

So, having a healthy balance of opinions from both sexes is worth it.

- You have reached a crossroad -

CHAPTER 9

THE CHOICE, YOUR CHOICE

85

To be single or not to be single, now that is a good question.

It is true to say that these days nobody has to really stay true to this single status anymore. For with all the dating sites, speed dating events or apps out there that allows you to swipe to the left and to the right, there always becomes an opportunity to be 'Hooked up' and start dating someone somewhere.
But I guess the other question is this, besides all the above, what would be your authentic intentions to not being single anymore? Would you find what you are truly looking for and choose correctly or incorrectly and what is your motivation towards not being single, could it be: loneliness, companionship, fun or the good 'ole' love?
That's why really getting to know you first is always the best initial steps that any single person can ever make.

Easy on the rushing, remember what we learnt in Chapter 4 on waiting, it's best to wait than to jump into something you know good and well you shouldn't be in.

So, SAVE yourself, especially where you can.

9.1 If the shoe doesn't fit: Then the shoes were right but the person wasn't.

In the story of Cinderella as you may be familiar with, there was only one foot of a glass shoe catered to the one RIGHT lady, Cinderella. The Prince ended up being left with the one glass shoe after the quick departure of Cinderella during the ball. The Prince's heart was clearly captured by her presence and all that they shared. However, on his search, despite all efforts to find the right lady amongst all the wrong ladies that presented their foot. It still did not fit.

Until that one moment, that precise moment when the RIGHT foot was inserted into the one glass shoe, the story became ALIVE, it fitted perfectly, just right for Cinderella and also for the Prince. Cinderella wasn't even looking 100% to be found. She had an idea of the fact that her shoe was gone, but even her evil stepmother tried to prevent her from seeing if her foot will fit into the shoe, Ummm, interesting right?

So let's flip it here and bring it home. So the Prince didn't give up on his search for the lady that fitted the correct shoe. He didn't settle for the ladies that nearly fitted the shoe, he knew what he wanted and with determination, he found 'the one'. This is the same for us too. If the shoe doesn't fit, then the problem wasn't with the type of shoe/s, it was with the type of person.

The Process: Living the singles journey as it happens

I had a really good friend let's call him Harry. We worked together and it was such fun, yes he was good looking, but of course, I thought he wouldn't be interested in someone like me, plus we were already friends. He had a good sense of humour and was so easy to talk to. Don't you just love when individuals are so easy to talk to? The conversation just becomes so natural.

So when I first met Harry, I did have a little crush on him, but that was that; later on, I found out that he was also a Christian, went to church and even joined in one of our work Bible study/prayer time we had, ding, ding and ding.
But yet still I never thought he was interested in me no matter how much more we were getting to know each other. So, of course, I carried on being friends, and to be honest, there was no hidden agenda as like I said he was a good friend after all, especially in that type of working environment that we were both in.

Months turned into years and we would catch up with each other from time to time. I knew Harry was interested in others as well as me at the time so that was that. We would talk to each other about our single lives, laugh a bit, and give each other advice and then walk away into our separate working world (desks).
He then showed interest in my lovely friend Tanya, I really couldn't blame him, she was beautiful and I somewhat encouraged it as if anything I wanted them both to be happy. To cut this part of the story short, it (their relationship) unfortunately, did not work out; it was a real shame actually as I thought they would have made a lovely couple, considering they had a few things in common, loved the Lord and all that other good stuff. But for my friend Tanya, Harry just didn't fit the shoe she was carrying.

The good news is that Tanya, later on, dared herself to open her heart to another prince (keeping in the Cinderella mode) and is now in a wonderful committed relationship.

As time went by, Harry and I continued to talk, about what worked with him and Tanya and what didn't. I think deep down he still missed her at the time.

Harry and I rarely met outside of the work office so when I decided to leave the company, I remembered saying to him *"Don't be a stranger, let's continue to stay friends and keep in touch"*. His response *"Yes, I will"*.

Fast forward; to nowadays I was having one of my mid-season moments. I realised; oh my gosh, I am still interested in Harry, but why and how? To be honest, at this point in my single life, I knew why….He was the only guy around that matched up to what I was thinking that I was looking for in a man to, later on, hoping he be my husband. He was a Christian and more so yep, He was in my focus.

So what did I do, I messaged him, it was one of the most awkward feelings ever, almost like deep down my heart was saying don't do it, don't open your feelings. But nope, I didn't listen and as I like to dare myself from time to time, I went around all the words but finally got to the point of saying*: "What if we were to date?"* Harry response: *"What you and me?"* My response: *"Yep"*, Harry response: *"Sorry I don't see you in that way"*. Gulp!!!!!! Yikes, my response was along the lines of, *"no worries at all, forget I said anything"*. (Hands over the eyes moment)

I tried hard to brush off that feeling, you know the big 'R' feeling, yep, Rejection, and it laughed in my face. His glass shoe clearly didn't fit me and the shoes that I had for him clearly didn't fit him either…what a shame, what a rejection. Another card was dealt.

Yes, I should have followed my gut feeling, that deep feeling I felt inside not to bother, it was almost like God trying to save me from this form of 'rejection', however, clearly, I did not listen and gave into my emotions. For this, I had to deal with the outcome.

The sad thing in all of this is since then Harry and I stopped talking. No matter how many times I tried to call or message him to genuinely see how he is doing, blank, nothing. I thought he was my good friend?
As time went by I started to question my friendship with Harry again, did I get it wrong, and was he not really my friend or was I just fulfilling a moment in his life when he possibly needed me too? I will possibly never know.

What I did know is this; my story shouldn't ever affect you from making a decision as I did. I have heard of other similar stories to mines and it has resulted in a beautiful relationship, even marriage. The choice of whether to reveal your feelings or keep it bottled up will always be your choice, BUT you cannot live in regret or fear of rejection.
Yes in my story I was dealt the rejection card at the time, I had to accept the results then, but as I said in Chapter 6, later on, I refused to allow that to be a piece of baggage that I carried into another situation I found myself in.

I have platonic relationships with male friends, and as I said previously I really value and appreciate their friendship, advice, loyalty and more. But I was also thinking, even if one of them was to reveal something like that to me, which one had already done, I wouldn't cut them off, as Harry did to me instead I would show respect for their feelings and still remain their friend, well that's if you are able to do so.

Here's a bit of content to the above:

Ethan had been my friend for over 5 years, we spoke every now and then, but were never 100% close, and we still held our friendship from the time we used to work together right until when we both left the company. Yes, he did reveal his feelings to me, I didn't know if he was joking or not, but he mentioned it more than once, so I took it that he was serious. I had to explain to him why it wouldn't work, because remember I was his friend, and I knew how his life was and where he needed to heal personally and more, plus at the time I was already in a relationship, even when I ended up being single, my perspective on dating him was not something that made me want to jump into a relationship with him, it pretty much remained the same, friends.

We had to agree that we both were not ready and in our single journeys still needed to do some 'healing business' and more. Plus I knew deep down I was not attracted to him like that, so if I did say yes, I would have been entertaining something I knew I shouldn't be in, a bit like with Tony in Chapter 3:2.

The good news is that despite that revelation we still remain in contact till today, we may not speak as often as before but we do drop a message or call each other here and there, which is nice.

So, coming back to Harry; I said to myself that I would try to contact him one last time, surprisingly he responded and we message each other here and there, and then once again it came to a silence again, things were never the same from that time forward, or maybe the reality was that I was just seeing who or how it really was much clearer than I did before. Did I telling him how I felt effect our friendship? I just don't know.

I tell you all this to say that as much as I thought Harry was potential boyfriend material, was he really husband material too?
Would I dare myself like that again, possibly, but clearly I would pray better regarding it, and not be led by my emotions or my type of 'season' at the time.

But then again come to think about it, Proverbs 18:22 (NIV) does say: *"**HE** who finds a wife finds what is good and receives favour from the Lord."* right? So, maybe it is not about me going out to find my husband-to-be, rather it is about me staying in my lane, fulling whatever I need to do NOW, whilst allowing my husband-to-be, wherever he is to find me in doing so. Hmmmm, interesting.

LESSON

The shoe may not have fitted at that time. But I am sure one day it will for the right person in the right way and time, so don't give up hoping for your wife/husband-to-be to come.

Right Turn: Make up your mind Road

9.2 Don't settle

Don't go choosing someone for the title, ring or to finally be able to change your status to, 'in a relationship', that you can freely share on your social media sites.

Settling to me is like having a quitting mentality and saying 'I'll just be in this relationship for the sake of it, this will do for now', whilst losing yourself. Doesn't it make you think that if you can give up on one of the most important things of your life, what else would you so easily give up on or easily settle for?

I do like watching some good old NCIS –Los Angeles, anyone else? Boss lady Henrietta says the above perfectly, *"Don't let a temporary solution become a permanent mistake"*.[19]

Why would you just want to settle for a mediocre relationship which may last for a short time, then after such emotional investment you may just break up and start the vicious cycle of dating all over again?

See, please don't get me wrong. I am not saying that dating is a bad move to take, but as mentioned in the previous chapter, I am asking you the same question: What's your motive towards dating?

[19.] NCIS Los Angeles – Created by Shane Brennan

I believe to avoid settling and dating anyone and everyone, I have found and learnt that we should date with intention. Meaning, as soon as we find a person or that particular person finds us, where there is a common interest in dating, we should date this next person with the intention of being a potential husband or wife, not to just date for 'dating sake' unless of course if that is all you want? But with keeping within the main focus of this book, we as singles are hoping to date from single life into married life.

As mentioned above, why not aim to look less on the title 'in a relationship', 'dating' and more on the type of relationship you would like to build, involving the type of characteristics we are interested in, such as love, self-awareness, selflessness, firm foundations, clear genuine views, positive changes, great communication, respect and much more, because without having this perspective the title becomes meaningless if no real connection can be made or established. After all, it is two singles coming together right?

Choose not to lose yourself, what you really like, need or value for the sake of pleasing others, because that my dear friend is not healthy at all and neither should be a part of any relationship including starting with a friendship.

Settling, I believe sells you short of what greatness you can achieve or accomplish. Don't get me wrong I know this book is mainly about singleness, but even with that exposure, an individual like you and me need to reflect on what really matters in our lives and what doesn't. And that is us being honest with ourselves, be it with our jobs, careers, homes, dreams, desires or even wishes.

I always believe that love should never be rushed nor forced and when it is, it's almost like you are setting yourself up for a disaster.

Songs of Solomon 2:7b states this: *"Do not arouse or awaken love until it so desires"* This is so true.

As singles, it is so easy to go all in as soon as a 'potential spouse' shows up with interest.

They may not be close to what you're looking for, but you say in your thoughts: 'oh he/she is interested in me…wow' and settlement walks in.

We may make the calls, pretty much say yes to everything even though it may put us in a tricky position with our family, work, friends, worth and more.

I remember having crazy dreams of which I married the wrong person. I knew in the dream deep down they were not the right one, but yet still somehow at the time I went ahead with the wedding, but sooner than later I had a wakeup call, said it's not right, was highly upset, ran out whilst throwing the ring down. It was almost like a scene from the film 'Runaway Bride'[20]; have you seen it?

It literally came to mind that with all the stories you hear, all the examples given and more, you need really to get to know you for who you truly are first as well as what you are really looking for in your spouse, because a lady who doesn't want kids despite the fact that you do, will not work, nor will a man who does not want to work and lay around doing nothing.

---

[20]. Runaway Bride – Feat: Julia Roberts & Richard Gere - Director: Garry Marshall: (1999)

LESSON

This is just to say, DON'T SETTLE, keep looking for your MR/S just right for you, just note, nobody will ever be perfect, we all have our faults here and there, but by the grace of God we work past those faults to be the better version of ourselves.

Try not to be picky but I advise you to have a healthy balance which is essential because you wouldn't want to lose out on a great spouse for the sake of not wearing the right type of clothing despite their attitude or characteristics being in check.

I know I wouldn't want to sell myself short of the best things that are to come especially within a relationship, so how about you?

9.3 Types

I was told that one of my cousins made such a profound statement, and this is what he said: *"How do you know that the guy you are looking for actually wants you?" Ouch!*

I shared this in my social group which was filled with only ladies at the time, as we talked about singleness and relationships and the response was like you could hear everyone take a big gulp in their throat and then the quietness came, yep, everyone was taken back by the question too, as well as I.

But, let's be real to ourselves, whether you're a man looking for a lady or a lady looking for a man, it was TRUE! How do you know what you are looking for actually wants you?

How many of us have the list? You know the rather long one that you write down what you want in your man or your woman, yep that one? How long is it, 20 or more points? No matter how long or short your list is, a list is still a list right?

Just to be clear, a 'type' is based on each individual's preference and attraction, and there is nothing wrong with that in my personal opinion, even I know I have a specific type.

However, I have come to realise that since I had made a checklist and turned it over to God for His perfect will and not my own, my perspective started to change, as well as my preferences. I noticed that what I may have thought was my type at the time of making my inventory is now not 100% quite the same. What do I mean?

Well, try to see it this way. We think we know ourselves better than God at times, but when I went speed dating I met some really cool people, I had good conversation with them but I wasn't attracted to them at all, however, I was interested in what they had to say rather than my then self not giving them my time at all to even entertain a conversation.

Yes, there is a difference between entertaining conversations, versus picking someone to spend the rest of your life with. But this is just to say that yes, I have a preference and yes I have my deal breakers such as being a real Christian, who loves the Lord with his whole heart, truly understanding, has a servant heart, loves unconditionally, handsome (takes good care of himself), good sense of humour, wants to be a father, husband, caring etc. but don't get me wrong, this is still part of my list but should not ever strip a man of his uniqueness too, because if it does, it will prevent him from being true to himself as well as him being true to me. The same goes for your list too.

Our lists should not also put a limit on Gods provision, why? Because any man or lady of any culture can carry such great characteristics, It's for us to give individuals chances to show this before judging them straight away, only based on culture or looks and this I have learnt many times, however, let me just say at the same time this is not to disregard the fact that we should be attracted to each other after all there is a lot that comes with that attraction, such as being intimate, showing affection, having children and so forth, so I am not disregarding that at all, all I am saying is that we need to think, really think about our choices before we make them. It's more to the point of whether we would want the one that boldly approaches us with it or not?

If I have learnt anything is to not 'judge a book by its cover', as you never know what gems are within its 'pages', the same goes for individuals too... Just saying.

I guess in choosing who you will date next is to be open to what you might or might not be expecting, in whatever shape or form they may come, without deceiving yourself of course. Remember it's not about settling it's about staying true to yourself and the other person.

When my cousin spoke to me about this, she said that she doesn't care at all what the person looks like etc., she just wanted the will of God and someone to love her and that she can love back and that's it.
It was humbling to hear that, but I knew deep down I wasn't there yet with what she said or how she said it, neither did I have to be, because for her and in her single journey that is what she needed to proclaim and do, her single journey was not easy too, but with that perspective she made her single journey seem so simple and pure and now she is dating a handsome brother. However, mines were different and so would yours and only you know what that could be.

I knew deep down I wanted only Gods will, but my way of expressing that went something like this: *"Lord, you know my thoughts and desires after all you created me. Help me to love and accept whomever you created for me and help him to love and accept me as you have created me to be too, prepare me for that time of my life as well as with him too, please bring my husband-to-be to me as I to him in your name Jesus I pray, Amen"*.

LESSON

We all have a choice as we prepare to move out of singleness. But as we are still going through the process, let's work on our perspectives especially as to what we allow ourselves to see in others. We all know of the famous phrase: *"Beauty is in the eyes of the beholder."* Through each of our eyes holds beauty about each person we see, and if we do not choose to see it in a particular person, someone somewhere will.

It's okay to have standards and values, and don't ever let this disappear as we all need this, but at the same time, don't let it be so unrealistic that you force yourself to remain in the single lane and be classified by others or even potential suitors as being 'too picky' and if you're like me, you would dislike when such words are spoken about you.

I have realised we can be so stuck in our 'types' that we miss out on all the amazing individuals that are out there next to us or around us.
Make a note, they may not be the race, complexion, build or have the accent you prefer to gel with, but their characteristics, their life drive, their deep longing to know God and more makes them so much more attractive than you can ever imagine. But will you be able to see it?

So I say, **'dare to see past your norm'.**

Allow God to develop you into the wife or husband you are meant to be and enjoy the Peace that comes with it.

'Love should not be a struggle, so don't make it into one.'

Be realistic with who you choose next, don't settle, don't move because of the 'fear of missing out' feeling, rather pray for guidance, after all we all need it don't we?

Left Turn: Solid Advice Avenue

9.4 Lights, Camera, Action

Rolling….Action:

I was on one of my church weekends away, helping to look after the children.

Bathroom break, on my way out of the ladies, I heard a man's voice say: Ask you what? Well, something like that, Huh? Was my response

I guess he was referring to the writing that was on the back of my volunteer's t-shirt, plus nobody else was around.

So I responded 'puzzled', huh? Ohh, umm I don't know whatever I guess.

He chuckled a bit and said never mind and went along his way and then so did I. What was that about?

He was good looking I must admit, the first guy in a long time I had seen on my church weekend away that I could say was 'my type'…Excitement rose up.

I had seen him around before, mainly around lots of other girls and I remembered saying to myself that I refuse to be one of his 'groupies'.

We had never even exchanged words before until that day. I did wonder if we were ever going to meet again, especially as my church is quite large in numbers.

But low and behold to my surprise guess who I saw speaking on the platform at my churches evening service; he was sharing his experience of the weekend away...oh my, was this a sign, that we are to see each other more...ha, ha, ha, it's funny how my mind was working at the time.

Pause break: Signs, we can get so caught up with others 'signs' and processes of finding their husband or wife that we try to incorporate it into our own lives and find it just doesn't work. For example, I remember at one time when I went to God about an interest and said God if he wears a red top then that's you saying it's for me, but then the person comes in a red and white top, okay, maybe God is saying something. Really? Let the rain stop before I reach my house, then maybe that's you saying he is for me, ha, it then drizzles....come on, we cannot play games with God. He is not a God of confusion (1 Corinthians 14:33), we just have to find out our own way of Him speaking to us and see what he says directly to us for us.

Pause break completed.

Volunteering on the next term, he wasn't even in my thoughts, guess who was volunteering this time? Yep, you guessed it right...the no name guy. Yikes!
Let's call him Sean. I knew straight away as I said before that I was attracted to Sean, but of course, I didn't actually know him at all, so I made it my goal to figure out a few things about him. I mean after all we had a whole weekend being around each other, surely I would understand something about him right? Right!

As we continued to volunteer together I could see how good he was with all the children both young and old, even with the other volunteers too.

And no I wasn't stalking him just observing, plus we were in a small room there were only so many places you could look, other than importantly at the children of course.

So, anyway in my mind, there were ticks all round for Sean, there was a tick for attraction, tick – relatable, tick- good with kids, tick – Christian – tick – a sense of humour and there you had it, my then list started to appear.

We had exchanged a few conversations here and there and then before I knew it, the weekend was over, just like that.

I got home and he was on my mind, I bet I wasn't even on his in the slightest. Who knows?

I mean, after all, I am single and ready to mingle, but of course not desperate. Alarm bells with the single radar of boyfriend potential started going off in my head and I had to take action (Green flag).

So I did. I added him on Facebook and that's where it all started. I must admit, He took a while to add me and yes as explained before I was getting a little impatient, so I took my request back, changed my mind and then added him back again. Ha, things I used to do, did baffle even me (hand over the eyes moment again). I think my pride got the best of me at that point. After all, I did not want to come across as being needy.

 Anyway, so when he finally added me, with a smart comment I thought, hmmm, you're cheeky, aren't you. But obviously, in my mind, I said I would give him a chance, benefit of a doubt type of thinking. In all fairness, I was still getting to know him. (But already making excuses for him ...amber flag)

One thing I must add before I continue is this? (Sometimes, people show you their true colours earlier in any relationship you choose to entertain, be it friendships or a relationship; it's up to you to see it earlier or later).

Moving on, at the time my bold, ready to drop the single card mindset came out and so I expressed my interest to Sean. In which he replied, *"but you don't even know me"*, dah, I know that's why I sent you a friends request... To get to know you!

Maybe that was him already trying to say no thanks? Who knows?

Fast forward again, somehow we exchanged numbers. We had even met up from time to time, sometimes more pleasant than others.

I remember our first meet up was at a restaurant, we both didn't know was a favourite to both of us. Nice. We had some similar interest, was this a date? He made some date comments, but to be honest, nothing was really 100% clear with Sean. It was pretty much, what you see is what you got, whether real or not. Trying to figure him out was like finding gold. But not being in the knowing areas was like being in a black hole...blah. A place I didn't want to be in either (Amber flag).

I called, he called, I texted he texted or WhatsApp. But then it dawned on me. Sean seemed 40% likely or willing to message or call me if I had not done it first.

We never kissed, held hands, slept together or anything like that so there really wasn't any hold or connection (attachment) in that way, but on my side, there were emotions and time dedicated mainly to him.

We had exchanged a few heartfelt conversations and I was honoured that he could be open like that to me, I felt special and that we were getting somewhere. I even remembered a time when he said: *"You are the only person that really gets me"* I was touched. But, was he talking from emotions or just trying to 'speech me' I don't know.

Reality hit me again; he never actually said Faith I like you and would like to date you. We were going with the flow, but that flow was very confusing and at times one-sided, even if it was a friendship. I felt I was the only one in the ring fighting for our so-called friendship whilst he sat on the side line, clapping.

I guess he was so caught up in the hustle and bustle of life that he never really had time for me let alone some of his other friends and family too, well so I thought from what I could see.

I wanted someone who would invest and make time for me as I would them, maybe I just wanted more, and he wanted less, and this was the reality.

As time moved forward and did not wait for neither me nor him our friendship was drawing apart. It really felt like he wanted to push me away despite all the effect I was making to say I was still around. But why? The way he started to behave and the things he started to say was just not always pleasant and he would turn most things I said around as if I was judging him, but truly I wasn't at all.

I get it, I really did, sometimes we go through things and push people away, most times not intentionally, but it can come across that way. I guess at the time I still didn't 100% understand Sean and his own inner battles he was facing too.

I really cared for him and I honestly thought I was trying to support him, willing to stand by him in the best way I knew how, but somehow I guess, he did not see it that way?

As hard as it may sound, you may just come to realise that in all your efforts your support may not have been needed. Go figure.

Funny enough at this point of time I felt like giving up and walking away from what I thought could be a friendship or a potential boyfriend/husband, my cousin always had the faith in him and believed in giving people chances.

I even prayed to God about him asking if he was the one for me. I think in my mind I was hearing a yes because my emotions where getting caught up once again (Red flag) and plus I really wanted it to work, but really in the silence God was saying something else, more like maybe a no?

I am convinced that it could have worked out beautifully if he allowed it too, well maybe.

Things started coming together over time of getting to know each other, but one thing I had to remember is that everyone has FREE WILL to make their own choices no matter what God says to them and you cannot force anyone to like you at all.

I am not 100% sure of what he chose, but I do know for certain he didn't choose me in that way.

The crazy thing is that as much as I wanted to be in a relationship with him and be his lovely lady, even trying to build a solid friendship was challenging, so how else was I hoping that a relationship towards marriage would have worked out?

It's a shame because over time we stopped speaking to each other, similar to Henry. No calls, no messages at all.

The most we said to each other was Happy Birthday at the beginning of the year of 2017 with his final response of your standard emoji's. Go figure.

Fast forward a few months and out of nowhere he appears at the same service I attended, I mean it's been nearly a year since I had seen Sean. We exchanged a big long hug and when the day was over and time was not on my side (which always goes so quickly for me), I began the cycle of communication with him again. He responded, I responded, but then it dawned on me, that what was going on was what used to happen before, nothing had really changed.

Was I overly hopeful in this area or was I just wishing that things will be better? Maybe both. The rest is pretty much history. I can honestly say that I do not 100% know where this type of 'friendship' is going, but time will tell, I really do not dislike Sean at all, his ways after a few years of being around him I had to realise just took a bit of getting used too.

It's a bit like the Marmite spread situation – you either love it or hate it (hate is a strong word, so let's say dislike). I respect him and I know he respects me despite our difference.

Sometimes as singles, when we see a potential companion we always like to make it work and there is nothing wrong in doing so. But personally, I had to have a light bulb moment along the way, where my self-worth, integrity and values shined brighter for attention than the single card of being alone or being in a relationship where I could be mistreated.

Especially when what is important to me was my self-worth, which I felt was starting to be challenged.

I had to wake up and make the RIGHT choice for me and hope for the best, whether I was holding the single card for longer or not.

LESSON

One thing I know is that I don't regret meeting or trying to get to know Sean because truly I learnt a lot about myself through the process and also about him.

The other important thing I also learnt was NOT to lose sight of who I am, no matter how anybody will treat me. Know your worth and your values and don't drop your standards for the sake of being in a relationship.

Today, I can finally say that I know where I stand with Sean. Yes, we are friends again. Ha. Our conversations are good and I honestly choose to accept him for who he is and know if I call or message him, he will always show me respect as well as I show him.

I no longer hope for a relationship with him in the sense of being my husband, but rather I am trying to make sure I am a good friend to him as I would want anyone to be a good friend to me.

No one really knows what the future holds for each one of us but we can rest assure that one day our husbands and wives where ever they are will accept us just the way we are, with both flaws and imperfection.

The Process: Living the singles journey as it happens

As I said in the beginning, both men and female will show you signs of whether you really need to pursue a friendship or relationship with them or not. Choose wisely and don't be led by your emotions.

The End

(Black screen appears, credits start rolling)

6th Stop: Prayer lane

CHAPTER 10

THE PRAYER ROOM

10. The battles are not yours to fight alone

The English Oxford Living Dictionaries defines <u>prayer</u> like this:

prayer:

NOUN

1. A solemn request for help or expression of thanks addressed to God or another deity.

1.1. **(prayers)** A religious service, especially a regular one, at which people gather in order to pray together.

1.2 An earnest hope or wish.

Watching the 'War Room'[21] with (American author, wife, mother, motivational speaker, actress, Christian evangelist) Priscilla Shirer (PS) was a big eye opener to me and I highly recommend you all watch it too.

Don't worry, in case you do want to watch it and are screaming 'Faith don't spoil it for me', I'll try my best not to. Highlighting the 'Try' bit.

The movie, in a nutshell, shows PS otherwise known in the movie as Elizabeth Jordan being advised to set up a prayer room to pray about all the things that are happening in her household especially with her husband.

---

21. War Room (2015) – Directed, co-written and produced by Stephen and Alex Kendrick

Towards the end of the movie, it teaches us that no matter how you pray, when you do pray, to God, He hears and PRAYER CHANGES THINGS.

As I said in Chapter 4, be careful what you pray for, for at the right time (in due season) it can be answered.

I say this because being single, for me is truly where my faith has been tested, but at the same time has developed me to be stronger. So let's go to church for this moment; The Bible says, *'when we draw near to God (In prayer, worship etc.) He will draw near to us….'* (Paraphrased James 4:8)

The same as in Proverbs 3:5, 6 (One of my favourite scriptures) that says: *'Trust in the Lord with all your heart and lean not onto your own understanding. For in ALL your ways acknowledge Him and He'll direct your path'*. These verses are so important to me because it has helped me so much, by taking my focus off what I don't have and putting it more on appreciating what I do have, who I truly am and what great things are to come.

Jesus for me is the number one person I talk to and take all my cares to in prayers daily 1 Peter 5:7 says: *"Casting all your care upon him; for He careth for you.",* He is the one I am upset with wrongly at times when I may act bratty and want things my way and within my timing, especially when it seems like nothing is working out for me, and He remains the one I truly turn to for reassurance of His saving grace, love, joy and peace for my life.

You see, this is not what we call, 'Faith getting all religious on us' type of thing, but rather it's my account of the personal relationship I have with my Heavenly Father through Jesus Christ daily. It is knowing that he has my back through the highs and lows especially in this testing journey of singleness and life in general, which can be very uncertain and sensitive at times. We cannot afford to be deceived by the women or men that quote Bible scriptures or dress nicely and say they go church but their 'fruit' (true traits, characteristics and attitude) says otherwise. That's why we need to PRAY; seeking God for wisdom and in depth understanding.

Being able to pray not only by myself but also with friends and family when I have felt alone, or forgotten, has always been very encouraging and uplifting. We pray on things, I have been thinking on and have been afraid to share, but also share relatable stories which help me to realise I was never alone, even when I thought I was. It also gave me a sense of community and care; I believe everyone on this earth needs that in their life. It is my sincere prayer that God will bring such a support network into your life if you do not already have one.

There is a constant war going on, we may choose to believe it or not. The enemy, yes I said it, does not want to see love, let alone marriages coming together and working out successfully and healthy, neither does he want you to be sane in waiting that's why he goes to attack your thought pattern (i.e. your mind) with falseness, doubt and at times fear. This is why it is so vital to get to your prayer room wherever that may be and pray always in faith believing that you're protected by God through His blood regarding your single path, your whole life, family now and to come.

Your prayer room as mentioned previously can be anywhere that you feel comfortable to be yourself, a place that is quiet and can be filled with God's presence through worship or praise, so that you can hear when God speaks (because He can and does) as well as a place you may need to speak loudly and don't feel you are disturbing anyone. Elizabeth (PS) in the film chose a closet; others choose rooms, church and more.

Matthew 6:6a says: *'But when you pray, go into your room, close the door and pray to your Father, who is unseen.'*

As you pray, remember Jesus partners up with you (See Hebrews 7:25) and helps you fight any or all of the battles and difficulties I have mentioned in this book and more, especially when you allow him to, at times we try to take all the control and do things in our own strength, but end up burnt out and ultimately lose.

'Prayer remains a powerful key!'

Just remember, you don't have to pray like others, nor should you compare yourself to others, as their prayers get answered so will yours.

Pray as you feel lead to do so. God will meet you where you are at, as He loves you ever so much and loves it when we include Him in our business. If deep down in your heart of hearts you do not want to pray on your own, grab a friend as I do from time to time who you feel is trustworthy and will truly stand with you. In the film, Elizabeth had Miss Clara which proved to be very helpful especially at the most challenging times of her life, especially when she could not see a positive change straight away.

There are also prayer lines which you can call up where a dedicated volunteer will listen to what you want prayers for and pray with you right there or you can submit your request on an online form. Here are a few organisations that support this:

The Process: Living the singles journey as it happens

- UCB prayer line
- Joyce Meyer prayer line
- Joel Osteen – Pray together
- Premier Life Line

(More info towards the back of the book)

You can even list some prayers points like the ones below to get you started in prayer:

- Help me to know my self-worth
- Not my will but your will be done
- I forgive……
- I declare……
- I let go of all the pain, rejection, frustration…..
- I receive your love
- Please send my spouse at the time that is right for me, not just because I want it now….

You can be as REAL with God as you want to be. He appreciates it.

I remember there was a time I had to ask God in prayer if marriage was truly for me. You see, there is one thing of having the desires, hopes and dreams to be married, but at times as mentioned before you really need to make sure they are not 'selfish' type of desires but rather pure purposeful ones.

I know there are some who do not feel called to marriage, neither has the desire to do so, and we can see this with examples of those that are Nun's, Eunuchs (See Matthew 19:11), priests and many more examples. However, deep down inside me, I believe that I am called to marriage.

I believe it is time we come to understand that marriage means more than just having a ring and all the gilts and glamour that comes with it in the few days of a wedding, so for this reason I really had to seek God in prayer and ask this question; *Have you really called me to marriage?* I also, always knew that I wanted to be a mother too, so I was grateful that even if God responded with a no to the marriage part, then there was still room for adoption if he said yes to have children too of course. But yet still I had to ask.

I asked that if I am not ordained for marriage for Him (God) to take away such desires and to reveal my purpose here on this earth and to have the strength to do so. Was it easy, not 100%, because I hoped for the answer I desired, but at the same time yes, because it was giving me the clarity I always wished for.

My confirmation had come in the simplest way: The desire clearly didn't go away; there were more opportunities to understand what marriage is truly about and what it meant to be a wife and also a mother.

Therefore, peace and clarity settled in, but at the same time I still needed to continue (daily) to pray for endurance. The ability to not give up in waiting, not to wait and sit around to be found, but to actively walk in my purpose whether 100% known or not, but to live, live life as I best knew it to the fullest. Psalm 37:4-5 *"Delight thyself also in the Lord: and he shall give thee the desires of thine heart. Commit thy way unto the Lord; trust also in him; and he shall bring it to pass."*

Our prayer lives needs to be direct, precise and without fear: 1 John 4:18 *'Perfect Love (in Christ) casts out fear'*. Philippians 4:6 NLT *"Don't worry about anything; instead, pray about everything. Tell God what you need, and thank him for all he has done."*

Jesus burden was real before He went on the cross to die for our sins and yet still He was able to pray in Luke 22:42 NLT *"please take this cup of suffering away from me. Yet I want your will to be done, not mine."*

I believe we to can make such an honest and genuine prayer with our singleness too, reaching out to God for help, knowing He cares for us and wants everything good for us.

If God does reveal that marriage is for you then your prayers should continue to be along the lines of preparation in the waiting. Asking for constant help to understand what marriage is as mentioned before, how to be the best husband and father or the best wife and mother, for your in-laws and your family and friends too, because overall you would you not want unity and love with everyone as two separate worlds joins as one?

For me personally, it even got to a point where I had to pray and ask that I do not intentionally date anyone that is not going to be my husband. Okay at this point I know some of you may be thinking, why on earth would you pray such prayers, but it was very obvious to me that I did not have any time to waste on 'going through the motions', I mean who does? I even had to pray against deceivers and ask God to help my mind. Remember I mention earlier about how the enemy and people like to play with your mind especially when at a vulnerable and sensitive place.

LESSON

Pray all the prayers you can pray, and continue to do so with a genuine and pure heart and I believe God will honour those prayers if not now, then some day. Do not hold back!

7th Stop: The Real Avenue

CHAPTER 11

KNOWING YOUR WORTH

11.1 Finding ME, Finding YOU

Beautiful faces ministries (BFM) was a group I started up a couple of years after I broke up with my ex of over 2 years. It was established in 2012 and now called Finally, I see (2018).

I had got to a point where I was out of a job because the company I was at, at the time was going through some changes and then redundancies conversation was flying around, as you can imagine, this job no longer felt stable, which made me single and living off JSA (job seekers allowance – It's a UK thing) and just about getting by.

I knew deep down I had lots of talents but the motivation to get up and do something ran dry.

I admired the way others were progressing in life but couldn't see mines, so I cried out to God saying 'What about me…'I felt lost, broken and alone.

At this point, I was searching for clarity, answers, something to restore my hope. One of my friends recommended that I checked out Heather Lindsay (A Wife, Christian author, speaker, and founder of Pinky Promise) blogs, so I did. Boy was I grateful as it met me right at the point of where I was.

I started reading her stories, experiences and journey of singleness and life itself, it helped me to notice my self-worth inside and outside along with how my relationship was and is like in Christ.

Over time my faith was coming up again, hope started to arise and my mind was being renewed daily. I could see the light at the end of the tunnel of complete freedom but yet still it was a glimpse of what was to come.

BFM became my outlet of release. I started to think to myself all kinds of thoughts, I would ask God for direction and He would say tell your story and so I did. Blogs came about, as well as posts on Facebook and my website was birthed, now (www.finallyisee.com).
BFM by-line was: Identify, Embrace and Uphold YOUR True Beauty. This statement was so real to me and I wanted it to be so real to others too.

For the longest time, I couldn't call myself beautiful, nor see it, because of all the crazy baggage of insecurities, lack of confidence, shame and the negatives things people said to me and about me. But once I CHOOSE to not let those negative words impact me, I then was no longer a caterpillar but a butterfly that was now able to spread her beautiful wings and FLY.

I wanted others to know that they do not need to give up on themselves and hate what they look like or what they feel especially because of what others have said or done to them, but rather to embrace and themselves for who they are and learn to love their imperfections, because no matter who you are in this world, as much as others do not want to believe it, we are not perfect, but we all are beautiful and handsome, you name it, all things good in our own special and unique way.

I started holding small group sessions at my house and what a success this was. Beautiful ladies of different cultures and backgrounds came together to be open minded, free and let go to be able to heal and start to know their true worth.
Our staple Bible verse was: Psalm 139:14 – *'I praise you because I am fearfully and wonderfully made...'* Choosing this verse was just to show that God made us just right, not as a mistake, but great looking with or without freckles, different coloured eyes, long or short hair etc. and we needed to embrace it.

Ever heard of that saying: *'How can you love someone if you don't even love yourself?'*

It's is so vital that we love ourselves but in the healthy way that God originally created us to be.

This is not an induction to 'How to be full of yourself whilst putting others down insert'; rather it's actually the complete opposite. It's more to do with knowing yourself so much better that you will cling to your core values, beliefs, likes and dislikes and not allow anyone to mistreat you or cause you unnecessary pain along the way.

Can you relate?

I know, if I knew my true worth a few years ago, I would have definitely faced a lot less hurt, pain and disappointments than I did through the past relationships and circumstances.

Being called weak, not feeling good enough, walking in others shadows rather than my own was some of my lowest points in life, but not anymore.

I now know through taking my stand that I am a priceless, precious treasure, not needing to be anyone else, but me. So what if I am not like others that is actually great news because I want to be the best version of me rather than to be a copycat of someone else. I stand unique, and you should feel the same too.

LESSON

"True love doesn't fall for disguises, it sees right through it, so you just got to be your authentic wonderful self and it will come" said mother Susan Landers to daughter Mary Landers in the film 'Love at first glance'[22]. I began to see this as such a good point.

No man or woman would want to fall in love with someone who is not being their authentic self. I personally would rather the man I end up being with seeing the real me and accept me for me than to see a fake me and accept that because there is only so much fakeness (deceit) that you can uphold until the real you decide to come out, and then what will happen next?

1 Corinthians 7:17(AMP)

"17 Only, let each one live the life which the Lord has assigned him, and to which God has called him [for each person is unique and is accountable for his choices and conduct, let him walk in this way].."

Or how about read it in this way:

(MSG) *"And don't be wishing you were someplace else or with someone else. Where you are right now is God's place for you. Live and obey and*

---

[22]. Love at first glance: Director – Kevin Connor, Writers and Producer – Kathy Kloves (2017)

love and believe right there. God, not your marital status, defines your life. "

So why not save yourself the trouble and embrace the real you. Your worth is of so much more value than you think; you just have to believe it.

Turn Right: Fact close

11.2 A Message to my BROTHERS

Don't worry, I am not here to give you a bashing, rather I am here to say I respect you and understand your struggles, at least I try too.

Ps: All men are not 'dogs', period!

There has been so much weight placed on your shoulders as to what you need to be and where you should be at a certain age and what you must look like or be like.

It's crazy because more of our men's are dying, fighting against each other or being individuals that easily give up because of all the expectations placed on them, and then your own expectations are not fully being met. But I am here to say, please don't give up, or be too hard on yourself.

As much as life is testing for us your sisters, we know it's also testing for you all too. I also know it's not easy especially when you do not have a mother figure let alone a father figure and your striving to find out your own identity, but you'll get there.

If you've got to fail at times in trying, keep trying because one day your failure will become a win, a breakthrough, an accomplishment, a hope and just maybe in relation to this book, genuine LOVE, first with Jesus Christ, then with your spouse and of course your amazing children, well that's if you choose that path.

The Process: Living the singles journey as it happens

If I am to be honest with you, in my opinion, some of our 'ladies' standards are plain ridiculous for you all, especially where your heart and your drive/determination is not even seen, but more your money, job, clothes (materialistic things) so I say look and see beyond some standards (not all standards are wrong) don't try to be anything that you are not to only stumble and fall into a relationship that is not stable and loving for you, because if you do, who will then willingly pick you back up?

Always aim to be the better/BEST version of you, living life with no regrets learning from each mistake, not allowing it to suppress you but enable you to rise above it.

You are NOT alone, you're forgiven and loved. God has got you and called you righteous, able, blessed, priesthood and much more don't sell yourself short. I can only pray that you will see your worth, your capabilities your talents and tap into them all to be amazingly you.

You are not also a product of society or the wrong that happened to you. You may or still do feel abandoned, lost, helpless, or even insignificant, like you didn't matter? Trust me, you do matter and don't believe the lie, you are not what-less.

Yes, we have all at some point had some challenging and testing times, and some folks may have declared some nonsense upon you, but it's for you to now take back the control and refuse to accept their negativity, bad-mind or 'only trying to help' mentality and rise above it and not give in to any of it.

You are so much stronger than you know. Allow your role models to be individuals of inspiration, reflective of Godly characteristics, joyful, peaceful and authentic.

So prove to yourselves that you respect each other, helping and supporting each other to be where you all need to be and just kick back and SMILE, and when a genuine sister (lady) comes to holla at you, using Godly wisdom and God's direction, of course. MOVE. Well if you want to that is (wink).

11.3 A Message to my SISTERS

Were do I begin with you all?

Maybe here: first of all you're beautiful, brave, bold & stronger than you think. Did you know that?

Too many times society portrays us girls/women fighting against each other and holding grudges, over position, men, careers and more. Heard of the titled 'Mean Girls'[23] why must that be related to any lady or persons at all?

There is this big old world that we live in and there is so much space for all of us to shine, so why don't we do so whilst helping to support each other instead of trying to maybe step on each other to get to where we would like to be?

I applaud you, girls and ladies that actually do support each other and refuse to see your sisters falling down no matter what race or cultural background you come from, now that's what I call true 'sisterhood', it's always well needed and also needs to spread and continue. Show some love.

People will always have an opinion about you, what you should wear, how you should speak act and the list goes on, but really and truly in this

---

23. The label "Mean Girls" is a tween expression used to describe girls who exhibit an anti-social behavior known as relational aggression. The term was popularized by the movie Mean Girls (2014), starring Lindsay Lohan, directed by Mark Waters and written by Tina Fey

journey called life, it's always been about trial and error but more about learning from mistakes and growing.

Don't let the world or others define your identity or worth, rather allow God's word that says your 'fearfully and wonderfully made' (Psalm 139:14) be a light to your path. Allow the words of Beautiful, stunning, gorgeous, amazing, precious, priceless, authentic, integral, treasure, unique and more grace your attitude, character and more.

Let's not throw any more pity parties or get depressed and question why am I still single or why wouldn't anyone love me or accept me, because at the end of the day, the facts are: You are loved, you are accepted more than you ever will know and just one day, that handsome man of yours will come your way, so chill and enjoy your life with all its hurdles and wherever God is calling you single & married to be.

Take a break: Connecting stop

CHAPTER 12

ENCOURAGEMENT

12.1 Stop & Think - Reflection

I said this before and I will say this again; you are NOT alone.

The single life can at times feel like a struggle especially when your heart is burning for love or your parental mindset kicks in as you look after your nieces, nephews, Godchildren or see the cutest baby ever.

One of the greatest revelations I got, was knowing that if God has put marriage and motherhood/fatherhood in our hearts then we can be reassured that one day if not today His plans for us will not fail us, why? Because I believe God is faithful. After all, he did promise in Jeremiah 29:11 *"For I know the plans I have for you, declares the Lord, plans to prosper you and not to harm you, plans to give you hope and a future"*.
Then Genesis 2:18 also says: *"...It is not good for the man to be alone"*.

People who may not share your interest will always try to discourage you or make you lose your desired focus for one reason or the other, but I believe you need to stand your ground and remain hopeful.

Yes time goes on and you keep hearing of one proposal after the other, or your best friend/s are now dating, what about you? Maybe stop always comparing yourself, your timing, where others are heading or what they are doing because their sacrifice, compromise, belief or actions will most of the time be completely different to yours as previously mentioned in the earlier chapters.

The Process: Living the singles journey as it happens

Seek wise counsel than an unwise, negative counsel. It seems so easy for people to flow with their negative tune in this season of their lives with the 'look at me' type of talk, but sometimes it's more about speaking life and getting associated with friends (old or new) and with family that shares the positive view.

As for me, this has helped me hugely because I know I can depend on my family and friends to hear me out, give me good counsel where needed and talk away feeling sorry for myself.

Singleness should not ever seem like a burden especially not one that should steal your joy, happiness, peace or hope. I remember at one point I was getting crazy headaches and frustration just thinking about being single. Wondering when it was going to be my turn to date, reading all the books, blogs, sites and more, to the point where I kept saying to my cousin in a breakdown, low season type of way...*'that's it, I'm done, I can't be bothered anymore, this is long'*.

But then I noticed even though I was in breakdown mode, my heart still wanted to love and be loved, I still wanted to hope and I still wanted to feel my happy ever after so then I had to shake myself off and rid the low season and despair state of mind and get back up again, so I did.

I even started to create a wedding folder, inserting things I would like in my wedding and more, not forgetting to leave space for my husband to be input of course. I am still determined to be hopeful applying scripture to my situations by speaking what is unseen into being (Romans 4:17).

When your single no-one ever promises that singleness will not be a rollercoaster of a journey, nobody even said if looking, searching, waiting in the right way that it will all fall into your lap. But I have heard and believe that anything worth getting or receiving in the best way possible is worth waiting for.

Going back to the film I earlier made reference too: A December Bride, Aunt Lauren says to Layla Begrudgingly a pronoun advice and this is what she said: *"Love requires a leap of faith."*
For me, as I mentioned before, because of my Christian faith, the single journey for me has been more pleasant than I know it could have been.

When I have decided to turn over completely this process to God I know that I can trust God will come through for me, it takes a big weight off my shoulder and it feels like I can kick back and relax, knowing He has full control and at the right time my hubby will come and so will your partner too.

Now let me just clarify something I am not saying I choose to sit down in my house not go anywhere or do anything. I guess what I am saying is that I am still going to do me, enjoy family and friends company and when the time is right I am sure God will hook me all the way up.

Joyce Meyer puts it nicely this way: *'You may not be where you would like to be yet, but thank God you are not where you used to be'* so powerful and so, so true those words are.

LESSON

It's best, in my opinion, to live life without regrets. You did what you did when you did it for whatever reason back then, but now take any experience, mistake to learn from, to be stronger wiser and smarter, because at the end of the day if you didn't experience what you did, you possibly wouldn't be more clued up as you are now, don't be too hard on yourself, all this I am saying to you is what I know has been true to me. 2 Corinthians 5:17 puts it this way: *"Therefore, if anyone is in Christ, the new creation has come: The old has gone, the new is here!"*

If you have never dated before and always been single then good on you, it can be a bitter sweet experience at times. So trust me in saying don't ever think you are missing out and need to 'follow the crowd' and test every guy or girl that comes by. All I am saying is hang in there and spare yourselves any type of disappointments or regret/s, walk with wisdom of course, even if you do decide to start dating.

Please, do not get me wrong I am not saying that dating is bad at all, because on the flip side if you date 'right', you can also learn a whole lot. It is more so how you date that matters. Even though for me personally I don't have time to date the wrong person and be filled with another set of baggage that I would need to offload (in reference to Chapter 6).

For you personally that is reading this would have to make that choice yourself.

12.2 It's going to get better

The year 2018 had hands down been one of the biggest challenges for me thus far not missing out the year before that too.

Two days before my birthday my dad was rushed into the hospital, he barely was breathing in our house, I had to do the little that I recently learnt from first aid training (which I am truly grateful for) to try to resuscitate my dad, but two-three days later on the 18th January 2018 my dad crossed over from earth into Heaven peaceably with such grace and humility.

After such shock and lost, my life felt very meaningless. The single journey didn't even feel at all like something I wanted to focus on any more, how was I now to think about walking down the aisle of a church without my dad by my side? I used to remember him saying that he will dance at my wedding (dad rarely danced) so I was looking forward to that treat, which now I understand it will have to be him celebrating in Heaven.

To me singleness wasn't really as important as it was before, nothing really mattered other than making sure I and my family were okay.

However, if I can continue to be honest with you all, one thing my dad always taught me though was to hold onto God, his words, his promises and use them for every part of my life, he was a living example of this to the very end.

A few other things that came to mind was that I knew that my dad and I may not have had the best of relationships, but I had come to realise he did love his family, especially my mum and those around him as being a

The Process: Living the singles journey as it happens

Pastor, it's just that he expressed it in different ways that I even being his daughter, at times could not see.

So, despite having the battles of grief; singleness, the highs and the lows of life trying to suck out whatever left of life I had in me, I knew I had to keep on going.

It's truly strange to say that when you have other things you are waiting or hoping and praying to God for in your life, how your single journey seems to become confronting and so much harder. And as much as you have tried to suppress the feeling of being single it becomes clearer each day that you remain single and then the idea loneliness creeps in as well as you having that feeling of 'just wanting to be loved'.

In the month of August 2017, even though sure, there were others times too of where I had a few breakdown moments. Although I had a decent job working in a nursery with a good team and many moments to laugh about, I was also studying to better my life, family and friends who cared and daily seeking to have a closer relationship with God. I still felt like a dark cloud weighed over my head.

At this point, I kept the way I was feeling to myself. I thought if I shake this feeling off, how I felt will pass. Nope, I was clearly wrong. It didn't, it just stayed and became worst. I decided to pray some more, being real with God and asking a lot of valid questions.

My work days got better and I realised having friends and family that you truly rely on and able to be vulnerable with that you can ask for prayer support was a BIG help to me.

I do understand when you may feel like you don't have anyone around like that, but trust me, if you look well, you do.

At the time my cousin had called me a few times and to be honest I didn't really want to speak to her despite knowing she wanted to talk.

We had a summer nights events at my church, so I went and it was so great, just what I needed. A bit of worship, the word on PEACE through all situations and then prayer, boy did that help.

Fast forward, I felt better once again but still couldn't shake the heaviness I was feeling. Things in my physical eyes had not changed and yes some say change takes time and doesn't happen overnight, but in my mind, I was saying why not?

I do like my conversations with my cousin, who later on I did end up speaking too. As in many of our conversations we try our best to be real with each other, share many views together but most of all we challenge each other to trust God a little further than we already did. Whilst daring to believe that he will come through, as within both of our hearts we knew Jesus is REAL and how faithful to his promises He is.

I say all this to make this point: Despite your single journey and all that comes with that it's so easy to feel even worse about your life especially if you're not at the place that you would like to be, and had a few tragedies happen to you as I did along the way.

Life will always continue to throw all its challenges your way but the question is, how do you deal with them?

Before you find your spouse you may want to find yourself and be altogether so that you have lots to talk and develop with each other, well at least that's what I thought. But at the same time, what kind of crazy pressure was I putting on myself?

The Process: Living the singles journey as it happens

It is right, to be honest with yourself and make goals, work on accomplishing your dreams and more, but don't put unnecessary pressure on yourself to do all of these thing to only hope that at the end your spouse will accept you, because regardless of this they should accept you on every part of the journey of your life, whether you are successful or not there yet. The same goes for you too with you accepting them.

My solution in all of this was as I mentioned before, is to keep on going. From time to time I could see people building their career, buying houses, raising families, getting engaged or married and then for me it seemed like nothing was happening. But clearly I was wrong and that wasn't true.

You see, as I said before, we cannot be so fixated on everyone else's success and accomplishments that we miss seeing our own. Neither can we be so fixated on what we do not have that we become blind to see what we are already blessed to have.
Your time, like my mum, would always say to me, will come. As I felt like rolling my eyes at such comments, she was right. It was the truth I needed to hear and really accept.

My house, my career, my husband, my family will come when it needs to and I am sure it will be at the right time too, and I will continue to make my dad proud.

We just have to believe it, because what's the point of losing hope? You would not want your life to feel meaningless would you; no matter what you're waiting on? Neither would you want to stress or worry about things you don't always have complete control over (Read Matthew 6: 25-34), so why not live a stress free life choosing to wait on Gods divine timing/will and all the other good things He has for you, for truly He has many (Read Matthew 7:11, Romans 8:28 and James 1:17).

Things will get better I tell myself too. My cousin always says that one day we will be able to look back at all we have been through especially on this single journey and smile, because we know we have come out on the other side, better, stronger and wiser.

LESSON

Allow Gods perfect will, whatever and whenever that may be, to be done. So let's not have the defeated mentality, rather let's have the victorious, encouraged and overcoming, successful mentality where we can finally sing some Travis Green, Made a way [24]song:

"You made a way
When our backs were against the wall
And it looked as if it was over
You made a way
And we're standing here
Only because You made a way..."

Turn Left: Hang in there

---

24. Travis Green – Made a way from: album: "The Hill" (2015)

12.3 #SpeakLife

"The tongue has the power of life and death…" (Proverbs 18:21)

It is so easy to say positive things when everything is going great, the weather is brilliant, you got a pay rise, you finally got asked out on a date, or you are going away on a wonderful holiday… I mean, what can top that, at this point, you are smiling from ear to ear. Your life is bliss!

However, as soon as all the above disappears or at times you see it happen for others and not for you for whatever reason, everything seems to change for the 'worst', all the negative comments, remarks, attitudes start to appear, but why?

There may be some of you who this does not happen to and you are able to rise up above each challenge you face with a positive attitude a round of applause goes out especially to you, why? Because it is not always easy, and that's me talking from experience.
Now I can say my perspective is different as I allow myself to grow and learn from all seasons but I get it, I get the struggle at times, it sure is real.

The Bible verse above demonstrates that our tongues hold such great power, just as it says the power (key) to speak (LIFE) or the (key) to speak

(DEATH), meaning we have a choice of how we use our words, internally but especially externally, do we choose to speak with life (positively) or with death (negatively), over our lives, present, others, future, circumstances and more.

On this single journey it is so important that we watch the things that we say.

I remember the times when it was getting so unbearable that I used to say things along the lines of *'Will I ever get married, no one wants me or choose me, what's wrong with me?'*

Some of you may go as far as saying *'At this rate I won't get married, am not worth it, look at me, or I won't meet my spouse any time soon'.* But in saying those things you are allowing your words to set up a snare against your life, present and future.

In the spiritual context, you can easily prevent God's blessings from flowing to you by just a few negative words that you may say about yourself. Personally I don't believe God will go against a person's free will especially if they choose to take their own actions particularly when it comes to what they say about themselves, even though I believe He will always give us the opportunity to correct those words or actions before the consequences kick in and there will always be some.

For those who may not have known, the Bible mentioned that God himself always speaks life into and over us? For example: He said that we are *fearfully and wonderfully made* (Psalm 139:14) when he created us, he said we are 'good' (Genesis 1: 31), *For we are God's masterpiece* (Ephesians2:10) so therefore, who are we to say that we are not good enough for each other?

The Process: Living the singles journey as it happens

In knowing all the above, the truth still stands, our words need to change for the better (to bring life) and not the worst (to bring death). Our words need to become more positive?

So, instead of saying those negative things, Why not start saying things the correct way such as:

"I will get married one day and it will be great.

I am worth it and my spouse will be blessed to have me as their companion as I with them.

I will meet my spouse and she/he will see me and accept me as I will them. No matter what challenges come my way I will rise above it.

I will not be stuck in the single world all my life nor be stuck in a rut anymore. I can do great things now and always, so I wait patiently with expectation for Gods BEST for me".

I am sure you can think of so much more positive things you can say, but believe, by changing your words for the better you will see such a refreshing difference. It may not happen overnight or it may just. It's all down to you, so go on try speaking LIFE into your life now.

In our Beautiful Faces group, We always tried to have a good theme running throughout the year; in 2016 our theme was on Hope and in 2017-18 it has been on speaking life inspired by my visit to my friends church in Canada, every month we had to write down things we wanted to speak life about or over, be it: singleness, marriage, families, friends, jobs, finances, health and more.

There have been a few challenging times when I personally may have woken up not ready to face the day, let alone wanting to speak or declare anything positive. But then, because of the encouragement, teaching and 'homework', we set for each other, keeping each other accountable, I had to instantly shake off the negative mindset as mentioned above and verbally speak life even when I didn't want to, Why? Because I knew it was the better choice to make as well as it will be a breakthrough of freedom to know that I 'can do it', especially in the type of world we live in today where all around us there is one type of negativity over the other.

It actually gives me pure delight when I hear something so positive on the news, whether it's the royal family marriage, dating stories, births or even a great life-changing moment, or a rescue, it always brings extra life to me, so if great news can lift you up how much more if your words and thoughts are also doing the same?

LESSON

Always remember it is one thing to think negative and another thing to speak negatively. So before the negative thoughts birth deeper to become outspoken words or actions, overcome it with positive ones so that positive words would rise up against it.

We as a group have personally seen the huge difference it has made. It is only fair that I share this handy daily tips with you which will especially help on this single journey of life.

So, as I said a little earlier in this chapter, I dare you to join us at Finally, I See with speaking life into all your situations, your hope, your dreams, your present, your future and everything else you need to speak life within, if I can do this, so can YOU!

I once heard it takes 21 days to change or start a new behavior, so why not start a new one today?

"My future is so bright I need sunglasses to look at it" I once heard Joyce Meyer say in one of her sermons, it got me laughing, but she made a lovely declaration and good point.

Now it's your turn over to you, How about you try it here:

List five areas of your life now or to come that you want or hope for a positive change. Go!

1.

2.

3.

4.

5.

Now place snippet sentences that speak life over those areas. Go!

(You can check at the back of this book for my example)

8th Stop: New Beginnings Close

CHAPTER 13

MOVING FORWARD

13.1 Accountability & Friendships

"Accountability the fact or condition of being accountable; responsibility."(Google and Cambridge University Press Dictionary)

Accountability, *a situation in which someone is responsible for things that happen and can give a satisfactory reason for them* (Cambridge University Press Dictionary).

As you continue to walk within this single journey, it's not possible to walk alone, unless you choose to, which I do not advise you to do at all, and here is why:

1) Having someone that is accountable towards your single journey or areas in your life which you face at certain times that can have unbearable outcomes can be such great support.

2) Choosing to make someone accountable in your life can work both ways such as how I am with my cousin and my dear friends not missing out most importantly my mum. I hold them all accountable, to keep me on the right track with my singleness, to show and tell me where I may be going wrong, or right as well as to encourage me along the way. But most of all to be completely honest with me, as I to them.

I love how the Bible puts it in Ecclesiastes 4:9-10 *"Two are better than one, because they have a good return for their labor: If either of them falls down, one can help the other up. But pity anyone who falls and has no one to help them up"*.

Most people who already have someone accountable in their lives start by asking someone close to them: Their mother, father, sister, brother, cousin, best friend, friend, mentor, teacher etc., its normally someone you trust and value their opinion, someone that you know will keep what you share confidential and not do anything intentionally to hurt or harm you, has respect for you and whatever you are going through but at the same time knows you well enough to be able to correct you if you are wrong, knowing that you will not be offended.

You the reciprocate, cannot at this point be defensive or always easily hurt, after all, you have asked them to hold 'account' for you, and so you should allow them to do so.

Remember accountability is asking someone to stand by you to help you either be patient in waiting for your blessing to come, such as your spouse, job, house etc. They could correct you when you feel you have messed up in any way such as sleeping with someone out of wedlock and helping you to not live in guilt or condemnation but rather in God's grace by advising you to ask God for forgiveness whilst praying alongside you. They can also be someone that may actually tell you to hold on a little longer to the singles invitation because they feel you may need to heal a little bit more, rather than jumping from one relationship to the other. They are almost like a mentor.

An accountable person should NOT judge you, make you feel ashamed, guilty, unloved, uncared for nor alone. If this is what you are facing, then you have picked the wrong person.

As well as an accountable person should NOT be someone YOU blame for your mistakes or wrongdoings as everyone has a choice to make and you should aim to make the right one and mature, so do choose wisely at all times, and if finding this hard to do, I normally ask God to help lead the way and through his spirit, he does, which at many times I am so grateful for.

This can be a BIG challenge, but if you are willing to make a more impactful difference, then this challenge will be like a walk in the park, with a few bumps along the way, why the bumps? Because you are human.

You could even try the prayer lines mentioned in Chapter 10, you could always call up one of those numbers and be determined as one of your challenges to always seek prayer in whatever area of your singleness, or life that you may need that extra support on a daily, weekly, monthly or yearly basis's, pretty much whatever really works for you.

Friendship, as briefly touched upon before, finding those who are really there for you through your highs and lows are the friends that you will always want and will be around.

I only have a selected amount of friends that I really share with and can honestly freely be vulnerable with, the 'amount' has not always been by choice as at times I have found that I normally want to deal with 'things' alone rather than be vulnerable and reach out, but as I matured and started to see behaviours and characteristics for what they were, I realised my true friends that were pouring good vibes into me rather than those who were draining me out especially within my most vulnerable parts of my life.

I always thought that you should be the best type of friend that you would want others to be to you and I can only hope and pray that that's how all my friends feel.

Having true friends provides you with an external perspective that you may not always be able to see about yourself especially when you are 'going through'.

So, choose your friendships wisely or allow God to help choose them for you, as ironic as that may sound, I believe it's so true. God truly knows what and who is best for us, be it a friend for a moment or a lifetime.

LESSON

Having as much support on this journey you will find makes the journey so much sweeter and bearable. Proverbs 27:9 puts it this way '....*the pleasantness of a friend springs from their heartfelt advice.*' If it wasn't for having my faith, my lovely and caring mum, cousins or my close friends to talk to, I am not quite sure what the state of my mind would have been at. Thank God for them all.

So get thinking, if you haven't done so already, who can you ask to be accountable for you?

9th Stop: Make a positive change lane

13.2 Stay in your lane

Stay in your lane and maintain it.

Too many times we want to keep up with the 'Joneses' or be like friend A or B that we lose sight of what our individual journey is currently or soon to be. We want to spend money we don't really have and then become in debt or have the notion of 'fear of missing out' (FOMO) that we become so far behind in our own lives that we keep up with friend/s who have their own issues or situations they are trying to contain or overcome themselves.

Everyone's standards are different and the morals (or lack thereof) of the world can easily sway you to either measure yourself by its own standards or view yourself from the perspective of others. Unless you renew your mind *"Do not conform to the pattern of this world, but be transformed by the **renewing of your mind**. Then you will be able to test and approve what God's will is--his good, pleasing and perfect will."* (Romans 12:2 NIV) or take each thought captive (See 2 Corinthians 10:5) meaning, think before you take action, speak and so forth.

Don't miss your husband or wife because you decided to follow the standards or some misleading of the world.

What is your heart saying? What is your current situation saying? What is God saying in the midst of all that you are feeling? Are you being led by your emotions or by His Spirit? Why do you feel you need not be single anymore? Can any of us really be ready for marriage? Self-check, right. How many of us really do this?

I know for me, it's something I must introduce on a regular basis so that I am not lead by status or what others think, but rather by what God is saying in my single season now.

Check this: I went to a Christian event some months back where Christian women & men got together to answer a few questions about life, relationships and each other.

To be honest with you I was taken back by some of the responses, why? Despite many of the responses were people's own opinion which I understood, it just helped me to see the mindset in the world today especially on the subject of dating, singleness & life especially amongst Christians. Some responses to certain questions where pretty much simply answered whereas there were others in which dragged on for a long time.

It got to a point where I started to get a headache; I had to have a bathroom break just to clear my head. Sounds intense right? I think it was because at some point in the event we all lost the sight of 'learning from each other' rather than shouting out debates of what should and shouldn't be.

There was one particular question that gave me a fresh perspective, and it related to the constant justification as to why women felt it right for a man to pay for them on the first date etc.

Now honestly in my opinion on this questioning, my answer slightly changed throughout the discussion, why? Because I got to see things for what they really are, from the man's perspective and how men really feel regarding this. It involved their own type of 'test' for us the ladies, their own confidence and much more. Boy oh boy was I learning.

I felt God reveal to me the narrow-minded view we can have especially when RESPECT and communication for each other become obsolete.
Take, for example, you finally go on a date with someone you are interested in. You BOTH have so much fun. The food and drinks were great and you both even go for dessert. You finally reach the end of the night and then the bill comes. What do you do? Do you both reach for the bill at the same time and each suggests that you will pay, or do either of you not bother attempt to show interest in paying?

Yes, the Bible says (Proverbs 18:22) *"**He** who finds a wife finds a good thing, And obtains favor from the Lord."* But surely it doesn't mean that we should assume all the time even on the first date that the man should pay? Everyone has their own opinion regarding this, and I got it, I really do. I just think it's fair to say that we should be mature enough to know if someone is just trying to use us or always seem to rely on us to pay for everything at all time, despite the first date now passed. Your wisdom should speak louder than your words.

Do not get me wrong, I am not saying that for each first date I am going to offer to pay, but I would like to know if I do, would I be stopped. What do you think (to the men reading)?

God did not call us 'fools' or gullible individuals with no sense', the Bible says he who lacks wisdom, let him ask for it and wisdom will be given (James 1:5) Paraphrased.

My mum always says in a nutshell that I shouldn't run after any man, do not break up a happy home, nor pursue a man, pretty much 'Stay in your lane Faith', over time I didn't get it, as I just wanted to be in a relationship then and like that particular person/s, so my then self will pursue and run after a man. But as a result found myself 'working' around the clock, putting in so much effect to just keep his attention, what for? That wasn't real love and that surely wasn't a sign of a healthy relationship.
At the time I knew it was a reflection of wanting to be in others lane as I just wanted to be in a relationship and didn't want to be left out. But clearly I was looking for love that only God could feel within, so in the midst of that, did I lose sight of my worth? To an extent, sure did. It's then When I started to realise that **mum spoke WISDOM**.

So what am I saying? Let's not get so caught up in what others think, say or do that we lose sight of what God has placed in front of us. Let's not make 'money' an issue before the foundation of friendship or getting to know someone is even introduced. We go on dates because we are interested in each other to see if we gel and if we can take it further, we go with RESPECT, dignity & integrity.

If we see any form of disrespect then we know what to do. Remember the red, amber and green flags in Chapter 9:4 examples? Come on you will know. God has given us common sense, right? Even in Biblical content, it says in Matthew 7:16 (NKV) *"You will know them by their fruits"*.

Who knows what the other persons dating standards are due to past 'negative' experiences, this could be a test to see if the lady is really for him, the money, or even the status quo. This could also be an opportunity for the man to see if the lady cares enough to pay first or is very stuck up.

This can also be seen as the women's test to observe, what level of respect the man has for her too...as you can see, it can go anyway or for any reason, as we can gather we as individuals have had our own share of experiences that become our blueprint for our future daters or husband/wife. So at the same time, we need to make sure that our blueprint is in correct check and not that of others.

Let's not complicate friendships, relationships, courtships and marriage ambitions. I believe we should communicate any issues or concerns as early as possible so that we can be REAL with each other with wisdom and gentle caution from the get go, don't you agree?

LESSON

Stay in your lane and maintain it. You never know who you may meet, date or even speak with, that could be your potentials husband or wife. Don't allow people's opinions to determine your moves in the beginning, middle or end. Seek God's council; it is always 100% right and go by His spirit that lives within you as He will always direct you according to what is good for you.

Don't be afraid to be different; don't be afraid to stand out. Don't be afraid to challenge the 'norm', instead, do what you general, honestly feel lead to do and then RELAX.

I now 100% agree with what my mum said and do not chase after any man as I believe he needs to find me rather than me personally go out of my way to look for him, nope, soz[25]!

I know my worth and not to sound big headed and all but I want to be seek out.

I love how Maya Angelou puts it: *"A woman's heart should be so hidden in God that a man has to seek Him just to find her."*

If any relationship is meant to be, then it will be!

Singleness is so interesting, and I am starting to find out that it is so rewarding because of the amazing gems you receive when many things are revealed by both men and women's perspective. I truly don't believe chivalry is dead and know that men can still show affection, kindness, care and love were they want to as well as women too.

Don't ever get it twisted, as I've said before, we are obviously different in ways but also very similar, but it is to understand our differences that allow us to really understand what a true relationship is and what marriage can truly become.

I look at some of my inspirational married couples around me that depict what true marriage is all about: including the hardcore elements, the serious conversations, selflessness, forgiveness, humility, joy, fun, adventures and the good old family time.

---

[25] Soz - Sorry

The Process: Living the singles journey as it happens

It is for us as singles to know that what we seek after in courtship then marriage is not promised to always be smooth running, but through all the development, tests, battles, wins and overcoming times as singles it will help us to be the best husband and wife we inspire to be.
So I thank all those married couples that I know for being the best possible examples of marriage that they can be, whether married for many years or just a few months.

Marriage works. It works according to you and your husband's standards, respect and values with a little sprinkle of help from those who have more experiences than you.

13.3 Position is key!

The English Oxford Living Dictionaries defines <u>position</u> like this:

position:

NOUN

1. A place where someone or something is located or has been put.
1.1. mass noun. The correct location of someone or something.
2. A particular way in which someone or something is placed or arranged.

Our position in life, especially when ordered by God requires us to pay special attention and yield to his ordering of our footsteps. (Proverbs 3:5-6)

In life, we may find ourselves in places or positions that we would never imagine ourselves to be in (looking with a narrow mind), but God sees the bigger picture.

If he placed you in the choir, prayer team, congregation, in a school, office, college, university, home and the list goes on, know that if you are walking according to His will then that is the position you are meant to be in. (See Psalm 37:23-25)

Who knows who may see you worshipping your socks off for Christ and it catches their heart? Who knows who may be watching you look after the children in your school or nursery? Who knows as you stand in genuine, pure-minded support of a friend in prayer, your faithfulness and care may enable them to see you as husband or wife material; you just don't know. Let's put 'singleness' briefly aside, this is the same with the affairs of life too. It's not about complaining about where God has placed you, be it a joyful job or not so joyful place to be at, but rather it's for you to ask Him what does He want you to learn in the position He has placed you in.

I don't believe that God will position you in places that will cause mental, spiritual and physical harm to you, after all his word says paraphrased: He will not give you more than you can handle (1 Corinthians 10:13) Meaning wherever he places you, it's to help you, grow and develop you into being the best version of you that you can be, with your cooperation of course.

I personally have been in job positions that I have said, what God, are you serious? But through the renewing of my mind and building of my character (Romans 12:2) I have come to realise especially when repositioned later, that it was only for my good, especially when I endured to see the end result.

So back to singleness.

Take for instance the amazing wedding of Prince Harry and Meghan Markle (did you watch it? Wasn't it so good?), now formally known as Duke of Sussex, and Duchess of Sussex. I truly believe that they were both positioned in the right place at the right time to meet each other, considering the fact that they both had come from 'different worlds/cultures', lived in completely different countries, but yet still based on divine positioning, their mutual friend (as heard through the television interview) who was also rightly position led them towards each other...and the rest is history.

Don't forget some important facts, Prince Harry didn't have to take a liking to Meghan; I am sure there were many other beautiful ladies at the same function, but something 'sparked' within him, something gleamed from Meghan straight towards him. Was Meghan so secure in her position then, as an actress, that she didn't even notice the breakthrough, the miracle, the love that was to come through Prince Harry? Maybe, well, I think she so was. Because as a result, she now is married to Prince Harry and expecting their first child (if not already given birth by the time this book is released). What a great revelation right?

LESSON

You may or may not marry a prince or princess, but just as Prince Harry found His wife, amongst many other ladies, so can you. Just as many ladies have been found by their husband, so will you too.

Please note, positioning does not always mean standing still and doing nothing. Sometimes God is calling us to MOVE. Move into the place/s that he needs us to be wholeheartedly and sincerely especially when it concerns our heart, our present and our future. We cannot take brokenness, pain, un-forgiveness, self-doubt, and fear into our new position or season. Rather we need to work alongside God and enable Him to freely position us where we need to be now and in the future to come, because we can be reassured that *"Every good and perfect gift is from above…"* James 1:17

So I ask you again. What position are you currently in? And did God place you there or did you?

Make sure you don't miss your breakthrough or blessings because you choose to be in the wrong position.

10th Stop: You have got this Avenue

13.4 Where do I go from here?

One of my favorite preachers is Christine Caine[26] who said this: *"You can't look to being over there (future) if you haven't lived or handled being over here (present)"* – (paraphrased).

As singles we can at times be so quick to want to be in a relationship for whatever reason without being in our current single moment i.e.: here, to heal, grow, learn, experience, understand, establish our worth or values, that we can easily miss the amazing process of developing into being the best spouse for our husband or wife-to-be i.e.: 'there'.

Tell me something: How can we point out the faults or flaws in others without dealing with our own, I mean who are we to really judge?
How can we learn to forgive others if we still hold onto unforgiveness, hatred, grudges in our hearts from the past or even our present?
Wouldn't these issues be dragged into our 'there', especially if not dealt with 'here'?
Somethings got to give right?
Choosing to accept the single invitation doesn't mean that you have to suffer in pain, neglect, rejection or fear of being alone, especially not on this journey.

---

26. Christine Caine is an Australian activist, evangelist, author, and international speaker. Christine Caine and Husband Nick are best known for founding 'The A21 Campaign' in (2008).

The Process: Living the singles journey as it happens

Singleness for you should become a time of reflection, closer walk with God, healing time, getting to really know what you really want and is looking for especially in your future, reaching many goals you lay out for yourself and achieving whatever it is you desire to achieve. Marriage might be one of them, but it should not be the ONLY part of your life goals, ask yourselves these questions: How good am I with my finances, do I care or do I not care, do I get easily provoked, can I cook? Will I make CEO, Director or Management or I'm I settling?

Check this out: Have you ever known that maybe your single journey clears your pathway for you to be great and do great until your spouse comes for you both then to do and be great together.

Don't just settle for going through the motions of singleness to then suffer in the end because the pain was too much, or the hurt was crippling. Letting go of it all is the most liberating thing you could ever do for YOURSELF until the right person for you decides to come to date again.

Life and singleness does get better, trust me, I can relate. Remember I am currently on the same journey too.

But as I mentioned earlier in this book 'maybe you just need to refocus and change the way you look at things', take for example: Have you ever thought that your 'want' has clouded your 'need' or views?

As individuals we can be so eager or caught up, for whatever reason, on what we think we want; that as seasons, circumstances and life changes as often as it does, we then find out that what we actually wanted is not at all what we actually needed. Go figure.

Be determined to tell your story of endurance, patience and survival. Even if you have to throw your hands in the air and sing a bit of Destiny Child:

"I'm a survivor, I'm not gon' give up, I'm not gon' stop, I'm gon' work harder…."[27]

Whatever you do, just don't give up; because if you do you may just miss out on something extraordinarily amazing that had your name on it, signed sealed by God himself.

Remember what it said in Songs of Solomon 8:4 (NIV) *'Do not arouse or awaken love until it so desires.'*

So how about right now you pull up your big boy and big girls pants, cancel your pity party arrangements and be determined to ride the waves of singleness.

Ride with slight caution, wisdom and understanding though, as some waves may seem higher than others, but they are reachable and able to overcome.

You may just see other singles along your way, some that are determined to knock you off track and lose your board, and some that will see you falling or losing your balance and will dig deep into the waters of singleness and lend you their helping hand, pull you up above the waters and help you to see again.

In that case to the ones, who tried to knock you off track, dust their seaweed off and continue to grab onto that true helping hand and ride the waves of the single life until the very end. Of course not forgetting to say Mahola (Thank you) along the way, and if they have to leave you so soon, high five them and say next round is on me, because you never know who else may need to hear your single story.

---

27. Destiny Child song: Survivor – from album: "Survivor" (2001) Songwriters: Anthony Dent / Beyonce Knowles / Mathew Knowles

The Process: Living the singles journey as it happens

After all, there are more beaches to enjoy, more waves to ride and more singles to speak life into.

Take a listen to my final two song choice; I pray it warms your heart: 'I'm Gonna Be Ready' and 'Still I Rise'- Yolanda Adams[28]

11ᵗʰ Stop: You have reached your final destination
(This Town is known for – 'Embracing its current season, whilst sustaining a positive change')

---

28 I'm Gonna Be Ready - By Yolanda Adams - album: "Believe" (2001) Writer(s): Yolanda Yvette Adams / James Samuel Iii Harris / James Harris Iii / Terry Lewis / James Wright / James Quenton Wright

Still I Rise - album: "Songs From The Heart" (1998) - Songwriters: Percy Bady - dedicated to Rosa Parks, and interpolated from a poem by Maya Angelou (Wikipedia)

AFTERWORD

You made it!

You've come to the end of my book and I am so proud of you.

Thanks for flipping each page with the eagerness to learn and dig deeper into a little bit more information about your singleness than you may have already known.
Hopefully you have got to know me a little better and I can only hope that you have enjoyed this journey and that it encourages you to keep on going.

Trust me, I understand, really I do. This single journey is no joke and can be very testing at times, but I want you to know that your journey matters and as repeated so many times through this book, you ARE NOT ALONE.

Be reassured there is nothing that you are going through or have gone through that someone else in the world on this same journey has not experienced themselves; let this be of encouragement to you that everyone has their own journey to take, but it's with help from others like yourself and I as I concluded where your journey becomes so much more pleasant than when you first started off.

The Process: Living the singles journey as it happens

Your life, especially your single life is all but seasons; you have a choice to break forth and take each season heads on and not let it defeat you.

My favourite author and speaker Joyce Meyer, put it this way: *"It is important for you to remember when one of those hard days comes along and you feel like you may not make it; it is only one page in the story of your life: it is not the whole story, so turn the page and keep writing."*[29]
This is so true, your life is not determined by the mistakes on this journey, because through mistakes you can learn from them, grow and move on.

So, no matter what comes your way this year or the years to come know that I am praying for you all, hoping to hear that your journey has become better after reading this book and most of all that you feel encouraged to know that you are so WORTH IT and no matter what age, race or gender you may be, there is someone out there for all of us.

Let it be known that your life is more determined by your hope, dreams, desire, willpower to not give up or stay beat down and much, much more.

So, until next time, Cheerio from me.
Hopefully see you again for another journey.

---

[29] Quote: You Can Begin Again: No Matter What, It's Never Too Late (2014) by Joyce Meyer

APPENDIX

Chapter Two
The Notes (Taking time to write: Reflections)

23 January 2011 16:06

"Life is always an up and down flow. But the truth and best advice is to keep on top and never let situations bring you down. Things happen and most of the time it's what we can't control.
God is so patient with us but at times we take our own roads and then end up with the worst result. I can be a witness to that as right now I really feel like crap. I mean can I really be honest. I feel like I have nothing but knowing God brings so much joy and recollection to know and have a relationship with Him to the point of having everything.

Things we see, experience and maybe even participate in can make us feel that our self-worth is nothing, but God has created us all uniquely. If we were the same as others then what difference would we need to make in this world and what would this world really be like?
God knew what he was doing when He created me and each and every one of us in this world. The question is, are we going to aim and strive to move in the way God has called us and if so what we are going to do about it now. Or are we going to make our own paths?

I know for me, a lot of things need to change. But most important I know that I cannot do it alone. And I don't know where to start. I feel like a mess, through the pain of my ex, through the miscommunications I have with my family especially my parents. My attitude has to change to be more positive and most of all humble. There are things that make me snap so easily and it's just not right. Lord it's only you I can talk to. Who can I really trust in this world?

I pray my scares will heal and that somehow I will be completely healed as to be able to love again, because right now a deep justice needs to made, but at the end of the day, who I'm I to judge?
I tried of judging and criticizing others. I'm tired of being hurt and hurting others. I just want to follow peace with all men, just as my heavenly father has told me.
Lord, let me not just proclaim Christianity, but to show the love & hope but most of all forgiveness to others as you have showed me. Lord teach me have to REALLY FORGIVE and FORGET. I really don't want to hold any grudge towards others. I want to be able to let go of the hurt people cause me and forgive just as you forgave me.
I don't want what others have. I want whatever you have for me.
Nothing is real in this world without you. Lift you head up women, lift up your head young man & know that God is here for you. We are not alone.

Freedom, love, care, forgives and hope is all in the arms of Jesus.

Stop chasing after everything you see. You might not have everything you want. But you have everything you need <Kirk Franklin>"

19th December 2012 22:56

"I wonder
It's funny Lord,
I ask you for a husband, I seek your ways and your face. I ask you to draw me deeper into love with you & I am happy to say, I finally feel your love & your care.

But Father I come back to what I said in the beginning, please tell me where my husband is?
I look at Joshua and think he seems like such an amazing person, got the looks, the eyes, height, the voice, from what I can see, the heart for you, sense of humour, a passion to serve and develop and also a family who loves you too.
To me he seems like the on point husband.

And I KNOW you have other 'Joshua's' out there but I don't understand how come you are not hooking me up?

If you could look at Adam and know he needed a help mate & then sent him Eve, how come it feels like you are not looking at me in that way.

Father, as you know, I've had my share of crazy, unfaithful, ungodly relationships and I don't want those no more. I want you so centered in every relationship I have especially when it comes to be and my husband.

For this reason that's why I look at Joshua sometimes and feel sad, cause I just long to be loved by the right person, your son, your child, your man that you have so molded for me.

I know his out there and he might not be Joshua, but it's still a nice thought to think it could be. From what I see you haven't given me any signs, or confirmation regarding my husband so how do you expect me to feel Lord?

I'm your daughter looking for answers will you not speak to me.

It fears me to think that someone who is not what I like look wise will say God said your my wife, when deep down in my heart I know that you know me very well and have created me in such a unique way.
Father, if you said to Rachel that my husband will be a fine man, and then I believe it and receive it.
Father, many thoughts come to mind, and as much as I trust that you will work everything out for my good and especially try to keep serving whilst taking my thoughts off this topic, it seems to gradually creep back into mind... Why is that Father?

Your Word says that you will give me the desires of my heart, but Father it seems like that particular one you have become silent. Will you not speak Lord; will you not come to my aid & rescue me from this thought of sadness which is meant to be of joy?

I know you can hear me & I know you can see me around this. The thought of that alone, alongside thinking that you don't want to move on my behalf regarding this is pretty upsetting to me.

I look up to you Lord and no one else; I truly love you with my whole heart and do not ever want to put anyone before you. You are my number 1 and I really mean it.
Father, will you not help me. I speak from my heart"

Chapter 3.2
Microwavable vs Oven baked

Love Language link - http://www.5lovelanguages.com/

Chapter 5
Standing alone (A.L.O.N.E?)

https://www.relate.org.uk

*This figure was calculated by taking the 13% stat from The Way We Are Now study and comparing this to the total UK adult population as per the latest ONS
data: https://www.ons.gov.uk/peoplepopulationandcommunity/populationandmigration/populationestimates/datasets/populationestimatesforukenglandandwalesscotlandandnorthernireland)

So 13% not having any close friends in The Way We Are Now survey would equate to 6,870,782 people without any close friends in the total population. This figure is statistically significant at a confidence level of 95%.

**All figures, unless otherwise stated, are taken from *The Way We Are Now*– an annual study of the relationships of over 5,000 people across the UK by Relate and Relationships Scotland. The study was carried out by YouGov. Fieldwork was undertaken between 18th June and 7thJuly 2016. The survey was carried out online. The figures have been weighted and are representative of all UK adults (aged 16+). YouGov is a member of the British Polling Council. All figures, unless otherwise stated, are from YouGov Plc. The same number of close friends question was asked in 2014 and 2015 (also in YouGov polls of over 5000 UK adults) and the responses then were 1 in 10 people had no close friends.

The Way We Are Now is an annual report into the state of the nation's relationships by Relate and Relationships Scotland. This year, the report is divided into a series of mini reports covering Work, Sex, Partners, Family, Friends and Disability which will be published throughout the year. The social relationships report is the fourth in the series to be released. For publication dates of upcoming reports, please contact the Relate media office.

-

Salvation Prayer:

Dear Lord Jesus Christ,

I am sorry for the things I have done through words and deeds and I ask for your forgiveness.

I thank you for seeing my imperfections and showing your greatest love for me when you died on the cross, which I may not 100% ever understand, but please help me to. I receive your gift of grace.

I invite you to come into my heart and help me to be the best version of me that I can be.

In Jesus Name I pray. Amen

Chapter 8
What do men and women really think? (Just the few of us)
With less slang used.

Q1. What did singleness mean to you before you were MARRIED?
    What does singleness mean to you as a person single or dating?

Q2. What was your perspective/view of women/men?

	Question 1	**Question 2**
MMR	Singles in the context of that via a relationship meant the freedom to do whatever I wanted with whomever I wanted (if I could get some attention from someone haha). It meant I could live life without the complications of an emotional rollercoaster playing havoc within. I meant that my pocket wasn't regularly emptying on dates and meals and other things couples do. It meant I could just go cinema or out for a meal with friends or anything social alone and I wouldn't be expected to have to pick up or drop off any babe. I was responsible to myself only. It meant I didn't have to text/WhatsApp that one person and invest my time in that one person. On one hand it meant that I wasn't burdened with the physical expectations of certain relationships that could cause me to compromise my faith. Though I was still conscious that I had to be careful not become a promiscuous hypocrite lol cos it's wayyy too easy to invest any time I choose in something temporary and carnal. Every now and then at a wedding or a social function there was a wistful thought that I wished I	At the time girls were hungry for great guys, and I could play the game like a professional. They need what they wanted but many times they irritated me cos they wanted a certain type of man. The good looking earner, the philanthropist, the Godly guy who still had a bit of thug in him and respected women. But 99% of girls I knew at the time weren't ready for such a guy. Many wanted the guy they saw in reality TV shows and Disney movies and ones that were on the outside great boyfriends/husband's, but they were not ready to compromise and settle for the friend who was everything their dream guy was to be and more. The older I got/get the funnier the situation got. Those cool friend zoned guys who used to fall back and let the Disney bf/husband shine they started to settle down with girls who were quick to recognise the potential and those who might have been a little more choosy or just wanted to play about and not be fixing up and getting their lives together were starting to get a little less choosy. Not in a bad way. But in a way where they realise now that good boy next door is now a man of God and has married the

	was with someone meaningful cos it meant companionship and friendship and as I got older it meant settling down.	thugged out Godly Hustlers might not be around anymore or he picked one of the thirty girls who chased him lol... I laugh when they say that there are wayyy more girls to guy ratio. But I feel like for all the multitude of Godly, hot Hustlers girls out there. Only a select few are ready for a real relationship...the Rest are still on their journey.
MMR	Well when I was single I was in the world, so I guess as a boy/man it is usually about impressing women, some guys actually said that all of life is about women so they will do everything to get women. There are different classes of guys, some who don't care about impressing women (gangsters and players) some who live for impressing women (sweet boys) and some who find it hard to get women. So depending of what kind you are your perspective of women would be different. I had a bit of all of them depending on the time of my life, I guess I started off in the don't care place because I was, then sweet boy, then hard to get then back to don't care, so it really depended on my mind frame at a particular time. Girls are often seen as objects because men are visually stimulated by women (women also by men) so that they see women as trophies they can get, I.e. in music videos women are portrayed to be assets... I have	Ok now, I try to see women as sisters and human beings, before my mind was clouded with a false view of a woman worth, as mentioned above. As I have sisters I possibly found it easier to have genuine relationships with women as friends. So in a nut shell woman are literally humans like myself but made for a different purpose. I dare not glorify woman or look down on them, I see them as human and Gods daughters.

	more just at work	
SWR	It is a season where I find out what I truly want in a partner and also allowing me to grow as a woman and prepare for my partner.	Men need to make moves...be open with their interest...lead...pursue etc. Yeah defo all of that... Largely the guy should be the approacher.. But I know nowadays it's not always like that, which is fine too. But I do think it's traditionally a 'man's role' to hunt for the girl (if that makes sense lol).
SWR	Singleness means to me a season of devotion. I get to be devoted completely to Jesus because I have no other responsibilities. It's a time of action. I get to be Jesus' hands and feet all over. It's a time of growth. I can focus solely on growing myself to make me ready all works from the Master.	That's an interesting one. I feel that single guys are wanting to get married, but they aren't willing to do the hard work that it takes to make themselves ready for marriage. A season of singleness for men should be marked by devotion to God. When they are so devoted to God their will align with God's will for their lives and their eyes will be open to who their wife will be. A lot of single guys I met aren't that devoted to God and are too caught up in wanting to find a mate before they become the right mate. I hope that's what you wanted. Lol.
SMR	Singleness is freedom and loneliness. You're happy you can do as you please but sad cause u miss certain comforts...	All I can say about ladies is I try 2 show respect to all ladies as it was my single mum that raised me , so on the whole I would say strong but each person is judged on their own merit
SWR	It depends what you have been through already.. so if you've constantly been in relationships then being single u will almost feel like you're free.. u only have to consider yourself when making	Men are like a box of chocolates, you never know what you're going to get. It's hard to say.. or make a statement about men. Everyone's different in their own way..

	decisions etc. Whereas if you've been single for a long time u will probably prefer the relationship and maybe see others in relationships and think u will enjoy having that someone to do things with. So it depends where u are in your life. It can be a good or bad thing... kind of like "the grass always looks greener" situation.	I don't understand most men. They should come with some sort of manual. U could see a guy that looks like the perfect gentleman.. all suited up and dressed well but can be a complete nightmare.. and u could see someone in track suits who turns out to be the gentleman... but us woman will probably go for the one suited up just because of the look until we get to know them and realise they have to dress to impress coz their personality sucks. I have noticed some guys do that.. they will have all the bling and designer crap just to impress because they can't do it any other way Not saying EVERY guy is like hat but it is something over noticed. I think men act very different depending who they are around. Like if they're with mates they can be hitting on girls etc. Trying to "act hard" but when they're alone they're completely different.... why?! Just be yourself all the time!
SMR	If you're asking what it means right now, I see being single as a bit of freedom. But that's after being in a longgggg relationship. I think it's different for you if you don't have options. If you didn't you'd defiantly feel a way about it.	"Don't be a hard rock when you really are a gem" - Lauren Hill The women (or perceived bitches) that act like they will eat a man alive are really soft

	I'm open to getting into a relationship too. ALOT of people get hung up on age etc...mainly females (body clock). As a man it's slightly different so I don't feel too much pressure. In summary I feel kind of philosophical about life in general. If it happens all good. If not, all good. Not everyone in a relationship is happy and the grass always looks greener on the other side.	
DMR	Singleness at the young age means.. Just having Fun.. Party life.. Dating with no commitments.. Being single at the old age is complicated.. Some could say its Freedom. But it's Lonely as a prison cell.	What I find funny is that.. You already know the guy likes you. But you will judge him by his words n action initially.. What you don't know is that poor guy is nervous as hell..

Chapter 9.3
Types

...Not judge a book by its cover, originally said: "Don't judge a book by its cover".

(Quote originality from: George Eliot and Edwin Rolfe)

Chapter 10
The Prayer room (The battle is not for you to fight alone)

- UCB prayer line (UK based)
  0845 456 7729

*Calls cost 3p per min + your phone company's access charge.
Please be assured UCB does not profit from calls to this number.*

Prayer line Opening Times (closed Bank Holidays)

prayerline@ucb.co.uk

Republic of Ireland 1890 940 300
Forces Prayer line 0845 263 7223

- Joyce Meyer prayer line

  https://joycemeyer.org/everydayanswers/requestprayer

(USA)

Tel: (866) 480-1528

Hours: M-F 6:00 am - 4:00 pm CST

(Canada)

Tel: 1-800-868-1002

CaInfo@joycemeyer.org

Hours: M-F 7:00 am - 4:00 pm CT

(South Africa)

Tel: +27 21 701 1056

admin@joycemeyer.org.za

Hours: M-F 7:00 am - 4:00 pm GMT + 2

(UK)

Tel: +44 1753 831102

enginfo@joycemeyer.org

Hours: M-F 8:00 am - 5:00 pm GMT

Find more location on the website:

https://joycemeyer.org/contact

- Joel Osteen – Pray together

  https://www.joelosteen.com/Pages/ContactUs.aspx

https://www.joelosteen.com/Pages/PrayTogether.aspx

- Premier Life Line

  0300 111 0101

  Open 9am to midnight every day

  http://www.premierlifeline.org.uk/

- Hillsong Prayer team

  prayer.request@hillsong.com

Chapter 11.3
A Message to my SISTERS

Research findings from: https://www.verywellfamily.com/what-are-mean-girls-3288579

Chapter 12.2
It's going to get better

#SPEAKLIFE example

(November 2017)

I have hope I have joy and I have peace
Today is going to be a great day
I am redeemed and forgiven
I will not doubt my worth
I will hold my peace; remain at rest, knowing that God will fight for me
I am not forgotten
I do not live in fear or shame, but grace and love
God is working all things out for my good
I choose to let the past go completely and get excited about what is ahead

.NOTES.

179

.NOTES.

ABOUT THE AUTHOR

Faith, A lady passionate about LOVE, community and God's grace wants to share it with the whole world.

Faith grew up in London, England UK and graduated from the University of Westminster with her Bachelors Honors Degree in Media Studies: Television Pathway, not missing out her recent qualification accomplishment in Child Care and Young person's workforce too. She currently works in a Primary (Elementary) School in London and aspires to become a great Author by taking one step and book at a time.

Being determined to spread the word of hope and encouragement to all, Faith upholds a ministry called Finally, I See: which expresses the need to embrace and sustain positive change everywhere you go. This enables her to use her motivational skills by holding sessions every month to help build individuals confidence and awareness by providing a listening ear to all that attend as well as helping individuals to find their voice, try their best to navigate their lives in the best healthy balanced way as possible by using as much research as possible with the Christian Faith as her foundation.

It is through her hard working, organized attitude and nurturing, caring, kind hearted spirit that she strives to be the best version of herself to all. Including learning how to love herself as well as others.

Faith's first real encounter of LOVE has been through her deep found relationship with God. She would not like to call herself nor claim the title of being 'religious', however, her expression of love and gratitude to God are through serving her community, spreading love and kindness all around, reading her Bible, seeking Gods face in prayer, worshipping God and learning so much regarding her Christian faith, her personal walk with Christ, life and much more through church, family and friends.

Being raised as a Christian, the youngest of five siblings, both parents served in Church as Pastors and ministers which did not give her the special DNA that converted her to be a 'Christian'. However, what it did do was give her the benefit of knowledge of the faith and a glimpse of what that journey or pathway could look like.
Finding her own way to the Christian faith through the Alpha course at HTB (Holy Trinity Brompton), and sound teaching from HTB, The ARC and TG Ministries church, Faith would gladly say, 'God LOVES me and He ultimately LOVES You too.

There becomes so much more to this lady than meets the eyes, it is demonstrated through her writing, bubbly but calm personality and so much more.